THE WAY
PEOPLE
LIVE

Life in the American Colonies

Titles in The Way People Live series include:

Cowboys in the Old West
Life Among the Great Plains Indians
Life Among the Ibo Women of Nigeria
Life Among the Indian Fighters
Life During the Crusades
Life During the French Revolution
Life During the Gold Rush
Life During the Great Depression
Life During the Middle Ages
Life During the Renaissance
Life During the Russian Revolution
Life During the Spanish Inquisition
Life in a Japanese American Internment Camp
Life in Ancient Greece
Life in Ancient Rome
Life in an Eskimo Village
Life in the Elizabethan Theater
Life in the North During the Civil War
Life in the South During the Civil War
Life in the Warsaw Ghetto
Life in War-Torn Bosnia
Life of a Roman Slave
Life on a Medieval Pilgrimage
Life on an Israeli Kibbutz

THE WAY
PEOPLE
LIVE

Life in the American Colonies

by Ruth Dean and Melissa Thomson

CONTRA COSTA COUNTY LIBRARY

Lucent Books, P.O. Box 289011, San Diego, CA 92198-9011

Library of Congress Cataloging-in-Publication Data

Dean, Ruth, 1947–
    Life in the American colonies / by Ruth Dean and Melissa Thomson.
        p.   cm. — (The way people live)
    Includes bibliographical references and index.
    Summary: Discusses the day-to-day aspects of country and city life
in the American colonies for a variety of people including members of
different professions, specific immigrant groups, and slaves.
    ISBN 1-56006-376-9 (lib. bdg.)
    1. United States—Social life and customs—To 1775—Juvenile
literature. 2. United States—History—Colonial period, ca. 1600–1775—
Juvenile literature. 3. United States—Social conditions—To 1865—
Juvenile literature. [1. United States—Social life and customs—To 1775.
2. United States—History—Colonial period, ca. 1600–1775.] I. Thomson,
Melissa. II. Title. III. Series.
E162.D39   1999
973.2—DC21   98-28726
                                                                          CIP
                                                                          AC

Contents

FOREWORD
Discovering the Humanity in Us All   6

INTRODUCTION
Becoming Americans   8

CHAPTER ONE
Immigrant Societies and Communities   15

CHAPTER TWO
Living in a Colonial City   26

CHAPTER THREE
Life in the Countryside   38

CHAPTER FOUR
Home and Hearth   48

CHAPTER FIVE
Crafts, Skills, and Professions   56

CHAPTER SIX
Science, Technology, and Health   63

CHAPTER SEVEN
Encountering the Native Americans   71

EPILOGUE
Life in the New World   82

Notes   85
For Further Reading   87
Works Consulted   88
Index   90
Picture Credits   96
About the Authors   96

Discovering the Humanity in Us All

The Way People Live series focuses on pockets of human culture. Some of these are current cultures, like the Eskimos of the Arctic; others no longer exist, such as the Jewish ghetto in Warsaw during World War II. What many of these cultural pockets share, however, is the fact that they have been viewed before, but not completely understood.

To really understand any culture, it is necessary to strip the mind of the common notions we hold about groups of people. These stereotypes are the archenemies of learning. It does not even matter whether the stereotypes are positive or negative; they are confining and tight. Removing them is a challenge that's not easily met, as anyone who has ever tried it will admit. Ideas that do not fit into the templates we create are unwelcome visitors—ones we would prefer remain quietly in a corner or forgotten room.

The cowboy of the Old West is a good example of such confining roles. The cowboy was courageous, yet soft-spoken. His time (it is always a he, in our template) was spent alternatively saving a rancher's daughter from certain death on a runaway stagecoach, or shooting it out with rustlers. At times, of course, he was likely to get a little crazy in town after a trail drive, but for the most part, he was the epitome of inner strength. It is disconcerting to find out that the cowboy is human, even a bit childish. Can it really be true that cowboys would line up to help the cook on the trail drive grind coffee, just hoping he would give them a little stick of pep-

permint candy that came with the coffee shipment? The idea of tough cowboys vying with one another to help "Coosie" (as they called their cooks) for a bit of candy seems silly and out of place.

So is the vision of Eskimos playing video games and watching MTV, living in prefab housing in the Arctic. It just does not fit with what "Eskimo" means. We are far more comfortable with snow igloos and whale blubber, harpoons and kayaks.

Although the cultures dealt with in Lucent's The Way People Live series are often historically and socially well known, the emphasis is on the personal aspects of life. Groups of people, while unquestionably affected by their politics and their governmental structures, are more than those institutions. How do people in a particular time and place educate their children? What do they eat? And how do they build their houses? What kinds of work do they do? What kinds of games do they enjoy? The answers to these questions bring these cultures to life. People's lives are revealed in the particulars and only by knowing the particulars can we understand these cultures' will to survive and their moments of weakness and greatness.

This is not to say that understanding politics does not help to understand a culture. There is no question that the Warsaw ghetto, for example, was a culture that was brought about by the politics and social ideas of Adolf Hitler and the Third Reich. But the Jews who were crowded together in the ghetto cannot be understood by the Reich's politics. Their life was a day-to-day battle for existence, and the creativity and methods they used to prolong their lives is a vital story of human perseverance that would be denied by focusing only on the institutions of Hitler's Germany. Knowing that children as young as five or six outwitted Nazi guards on a daily basis, that Jewish policemen helped the Germans control the ghetto, that children attended secret schools in the ghetto and even earned diplomas—these are the things that reveal the fabric of life, that can inspire, intrigue, and amaze.

Books in The Way People Live series allow both the casual reader and the student to see humans as victims, heroes, and onlookers. And although humans act in ways that can fill us with feelings of sorrow and revulsion, it is important to remember that "hero," "predator," and "victim" are dangerous terms. Heaping undue pity or praise on people reduces them to objects, and strips them of their humanity.

Seeing the Jews of Warsaw only as victims is to deny their humanity. Seeing them only as they appear in surviving photos, staring at the camera with infinite sadness, is limiting, both to them and to those who want to understand them. To an object of pity, the only appropriate response becomes "Those poor creatures!" and that reduces both the quality of their struggle and the depth of their despair. No one is served by such two-dimensional views of people and their cultures.

With this in mind, The Way People Live series strives to flesh out the traditional, two-dimensional views of people in various cultures and historical circumstances. Using a wide variety of primary quotations—the words not only of the politicians and government leaders, but of the real people whose lives are being examined—each book in the series attempts to show an honest and complete picture of a culture removed from our own by time or space.

By examining cultures in this way, the reader will notice not only the glaring differences from his or her own culture, but also will be struck by the similarities. For indeed, people share common needs—warmth, good company, stability, and affirmation from others. Ultimately, seeing how people really live, or have lived can only enrich our understanding of ourselves.

Becoming Americans

After Christopher Columbus sailed across the Atlantic and discovered the New World in 1492, sailors from many European nations set out west on voyages of discovery. Europeans were curious about these new lands, but they were also determined to find trading routes that would enable their countries to increase their wealth. In the 1500s the myth of El Dorado, the city of gold, led Spanish and Portuguese soldiers to explore the Aztec and Incan empires in Central and South America. Conquering the native peoples, the Spanish and Portuguese seized enormous amounts of gold and other precious metals and brought shiploads of treasure back to their monarchs. Only in the following century, however, did Europeans begin to learn what potential the North American continent might hold for them.

Although a few French and Spanish explorers and traders came to Florida in the 1560s, the colonization of North America began in earnest in the early 1600s. During this period the English king authorized two groups—the Virginia Company and the Plymouth Company—to explore and settle the New World. The colonial period of American history lasted until the colonies finally united and declared their independence from England in 1776.

By the middle of the eighteenth century, twenty-five years before the Revolutionary War, colonists had claimed most of the land east of the Allegheny Mountains. They were living in thirteen different colonies, all of which had come under the rule of the king of England. To the north were French settlements that would become the eastern provinces of Canada. The French colonies were linked through trade routes that went down the Mississippi River to New Orleans. To the south, the Spanish had settled Florida and were ruling the Louisiana territory as well. Neither the French nor the Spanish colonies, however, had great numbers of settlers. These nations focused on trading and exploration rather than on building extensive communities in the New World.

Why Did Europeans Come to America?

Travel to the New World was difficult, expensive, and very dangerous. William Bradford, who later became governor of Massachusetts, landed at Plymouth Rock on a cold November day in 1620 along with the first English immigrants to the area. In his history of the first settlement, Bradford described how frightened the Pilgrims had been during the voyage across the "vast and furious ocean" in the *Mayflower*, and how lonely and dangerous they found their new land.

> Being thus past the vast ocean, and a sea of troubles . . . they had now no friends to wellcome them, no inns to entertaine or refresh their weatherbeaten bodies. . . . And the season it was winter, and they

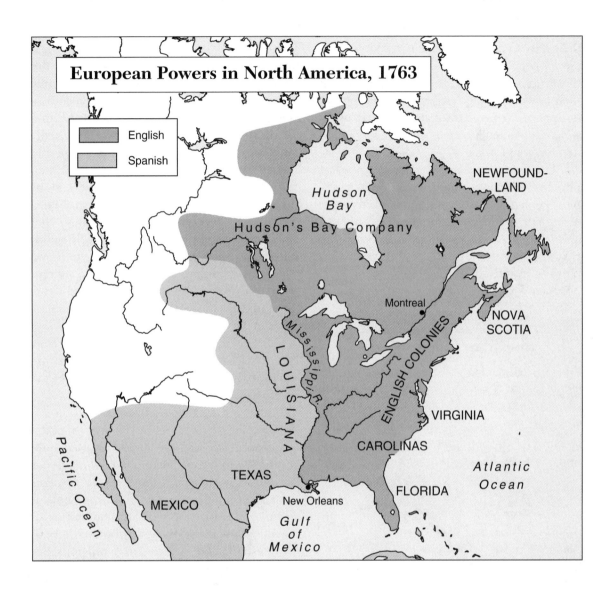

European Powers in North America, 1763

English
Spanish

NEWFOUND-
LAND

*Hudson
Bay*

Hudson's Bay Company

Montreal

NOVA
SCOTIA

ENGLISH COLONIES

Mississippi R.

LOUISIANA

VIRGINIA

CAROLINAS

*Atlantic
Ocean*

Pacific Ocean

TEXAS

FLORIDA

MEXICO

New Orleans

*Gulf
of
Mexico*

that know the winters of that country know them to be sharp and violent, and subjecte to cruell and feirce storms, dangerous to travell to known places, much more to search [explore] an unknown coast. Besides, what could they see but a hidious and desolate wildernes, full of wild beasts and wild men?[1]

Despite similar fears and dangers, hundreds of thousands of Europeans made the long overland journey to the seaport, embarked on the ocean voyage that could take months, and began their lives again in a different land during the colonial period. They came to America for many reasons, and these goals changed somewhat as the years rolled by. In the earliest years, the search for a northwest passage and the hope of finding great riches motivated new colonists. Other Europeans were inspired to come to the New World by their religious faiths. Some believed that it was their duty to bring Christianity to native peoples; others wanted freedom to live according to religious views that were not acceptable in their homelands. The largest remaining group of immigrants came for economic reasons: to support their families by subsistence farming or to raise crops for sale.

The colonists' early dreams did not last into the eighteenth century. European explorers had hoped to discover a river or ocean north of the continent that would enable ships to sail west from Europe to the rich trading grounds of Asia. A northwest passage would allow ships to avoid a long, perilous voyage around the southern tip of

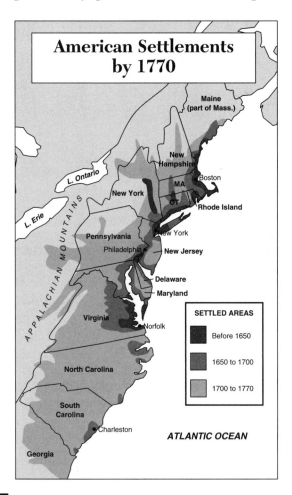

American Settlements by 1770

Maine (part of Mass.)

L. Ontario

New Hampshire

New York

Boston

MA

CT

Rhode Island

L. Erie

A P P A L A C H I A N   M O U N T A I N S

Pennsylvania

Philadelphia

New York

New Jersey

Delaware

Maryland

Virginia

Norfolk

SETTLED AREAS

Before 1650

1650 to 1700

1700 to 1770

North Carolina

South Carolina

Charleston

ATLANTIC OCEAN

Georgia

Africa or South America to trade with China and India. Some American settlements were established to support these explorers, while others provided supplies to men who were seeking gold such as the Spanish had found in the Incan empire. Explorers were finally able to establish that the landmass of the North American continent extends north into the Arctic, where solid ice prevents ships from traveling to the Pacific Ocean. They also discovered, much to their dismay, that the Native Americans of the eastern woodlands did not have great stores of gold and silver that could be taken back to a royal treasury in Europe. Yet settlers continued to arrive, to clear the land, and to embark on new lives in the colonies.

Many Europeans came to the New World with the strong intention of converting the native peoples, whom they saw as savages, to Christianity. This aim continued to motivate some colonists even though the effort was largely rejected by the peoples of the different Native American nations. Benjamin Franklin, who was the Indian Commissioner of Pennsylvania at this time, wrote, "Savages we call them because their Manners differ from ours, which we think the Perfection of Civility; they think the same of theirs."[2] With long-established cultures and religious beliefs of their own, the Indians desired little from the white immigrants, except the material objects produced by their advanced technological skills: cloth and clothing, tools, cooking pots, and guns.

While some Europeans came with a religious mission, others were fleeing religious persecution in Europe. Colonies such as Massachusetts, New Hampshire, Connecticut, and Pennsylvania were havens for religious sects that wanted to establish permanent settlements where their followers could live in safety. George Fox, one of the founders of the

George Fox helped found the English Quaker sect and hoped that in America his followers could live according to Quaker beliefs and be safe from religious persecution.

English Quaker sect, reflected the spiritual concerns that inspired many colonists in a message he sent to some Quaker immigrants: "My friends going over to plant, and make outward plantations in America, keep your own plantations in your hearts, with the spirit and power of God, that your own vines and lilies be not hurt."[3] Strong in the conviction that their religious position was correct, the religious colonists were motivated both by the need to escape from their hostile home countries and by the dream of setting up a new society that would be governed according to their beliefs.

Opportunities in the New World

Religious refugees saw in the New World an opportunity for creating communities where their views could find acceptance; in contrast, many businessmen saw the opportunity to make a financial profit. Ambitious landowners, some of whom already owned profitable plantations in the West Indies, obtained permission to establish colonies such as the Carolinas. They expected to make money from the cultivation of profitable crops in the New World, and they encouraged settlers to move to these territories and farm the land.

Not everyone who crossed the Atlantic found the New World to be a land of freedom and opportunity, however. Virtually all of the Africans living in the colonies had been captured and brought there as slaves. In addition, a very high proportion of the whites were indentured—bound to serve a master, usually for seven years. In 1750 half of the population of the thirteen colonies (excluding Native Americans) was living in limited or lifelong servitude. Still, those in bondage helped build the young nation and influenced its character for generations to come.

The Different Peoples of the Colonies

In 1750 the word *American*, first reserved for native peoples, was just beginning to be used for European settlers as well. Yet the "Americans" were separated from each other by different governments, lifestyles, and traditions, as well as by geography, which included wilderness, forests, mountains, and rivers. Few roads or bridges existed to make travel by horseback or wagon easier, and the difficulty of traveling often prevented colonists from coming together and getting to know each other. In addition, compared to modern times there were few people. In 1750 the different colonies had a population of little more than a million European settlers and

African slaves, mostly living along the Atlantic shore and inland only as far as the Appalachian Mountains.

The population of Native Americans living in this part of the continent can only be estimated, but historians believe that their numbers were declining rapidly. Probably about five hundred thousand Indians lived along the eastern seaboard when the Pilgrims arrived in 1620—and almost none remained two hundred years later. By 1750 Native Americans could no longer live along the Atlantic coast, which was heavily settled by people of European origin. The Indians who had survived contact with European settlers had been forced westward, and that movement disturbed and displaced other tribes as well.

When the Europeans arrived in North America, they did not enter a unified empire like that of the Incas or Aztecs in Central and South America. For the most part, the Native Americans living in the thirteen colonies identified with their own tribe or nation and did not feel linked with members of another tribe. Some tribes in the eastern woodlands lived in villages loosely allied with neighboring communities that shared their language and culture. In general, though, the different tribal groups had no common language and were unable to communicate with each other. Historians believe that more than two thousand different Indian languages were being spoken in the Americas when European colonization began.

The environment also created distinctions between tribes that were based on their lifestyles. In the South, where the growing season was long, Native Americans obtained most of their food from farming. The Indian nations of the North, however, remained largely dependent on hunting and fishing, though successive plantings of corn in the spring allowed them to make the most of the

Many different Indian tribes inhabited the thirteen colonies before the arrival of colonists. Here an Indian chief confers with his tribe about the arriving colonists.

short growing season. The need to control territory and ensure that there would be enough to eat often led Native American tribes into conflict with each other.

The English Heritage of Colonial Government

The English kings saw their colonies in North America as extensions of their realm. Each colony was closely linked to the home country, and the colonists remained subjects of the monarch. The English king gave certain men proprietary rights in the New World through written agreements called charters. These documents generally permitted the colonies to make their own laws and regulations, but these had to be "agreeable to the laws, statutes, government, and policy"[4] of England. The settlers were still subject to English law, but typically the charter also granted the same "liberties, franchises, and immunities"[5] that applied to other English subjects of the king.

In 1750, 60 percent of the American colonists were from England. Some were descendants of the families that had established themselves in the New World in the 1600s; others were part of the flood of English immigrants who crossed the Atlantic in the first half of the eighteenth century. Most of these colonists considered themselves subjects of King George, just as if they were living in London, England. They celebrated the birthday of the king as a holiday and drank to his health on ceremonial occasions.

Regardless of national heritage, though, no one at that time considered the thirteen colonies linked into a unified "country." Instead, settlers identified with their own colony. They were Virginians, Pennsylvanians, or people from Massachusetts. As Benjamin Franklin explained, the colonies "are not only under different governors, but have different laws, different interests, and some of them different religious persuasions and manners."[6] Colonies disputed with each other over boundaries, tariffs, and other regulations, while the political conflicts of European nations often spilled across the Atlantic and highlighted these regional differences.

As the colonies became established economic and political entities, the nature of their ties to Europe changed. Though some colonists remained loyal to their home countries, many

New Life in the New World

Michel-Guillaume-Jean de Crèvecoeur came to the New World from France in 1755. After traveling through the colonies, he became a naturalized citizen of New York and bought a farm. Crèvecoeur wrote a series of essays about life in the colonies called *Letters from an American Farmer*. In one of these essays, excerpted in editor George McMichael's *Anthology of American Literature*, he described how immigration tended to change the colonists.

"An European, when he first arrives, seems limited in his intentions as well as his views, but he very suddenly alters his scale; two hundred miles formerly appeared a very great distance; it is now but a trifle; he no sooner breathes our air than he forms schemes and embarks in designs he never would have thought of in his own country. There the plenitude of society confines many useful ideas and often extinguishes the most laudable schemes which here ripen into maturity. Thus Europeans become Americans."

In Such Misery

In 1750 Gottlieb Mittelberger traveled from Germany to Pennsylvania aboard a ship that was carrying four hundred people jammed into sleeping areas that measured only two feet by six feet. The ship went first to England and then to Philadelphia, a voyage of fifteen weeks. Mittelberger's book *Journey to Pennsylvania*, quoted in Richard Middleton's *Colonial America*, described the conditions on board ship.

"During the journey, the ship was full of pitiful signs of distress—smells, fumes, horrors, vomiting, various kinds of sea sickness, fever, dysentery, headaches, heat, constipation, boils, scurvy, cancer, mouth-rot, and similar afflictions, all of them caused by the age and highly salted state of the food, especially of the meat, as well as by the bad and very filthy water, which brings about the miserable destruction and death of many. Add to all that shortage of food, hunger, thirst, frost, heat, dampness, fear, misery, vexation, and lamentation as well as other troubles. . . .

All this misery reached its climax when in addition to everything else one must suffer through two or three days and nights of storm, with everyone convinced that the ship with all aboard is bound to sink. In such misery, all the people on board pray and cry pitifully together. . . . Many groan and exclaim, 'Oh! If only I were back at home, even lying in my pigsty!'"

came to resent the power that a distant government had over their lives. By the 1750s some colonial politicians were beginning to see that the different colonies had many common interests and needs. In time, these desires and attitudes would become more important to the colonists than allegiance to a kingdom in faraway Europe.

Immigrant Societies and Communities

Even in the mid–eighteenth century, when the New World had been settled for 130 years, it was an enormous risk for a European to cross the Atlantic Ocean and immigrate to an American colony. The long ocean voyage was itself hazardous, especially since most ships were overcrowded and filthy. Once in America, the colonists faced the challenge of finding shelter and obtaining a livelihood in an unfamiliar environment where the weather was often harsh. Yet decades of war had caused extreme poverty in Europe, and many people were willing to face the dangers of immigrating to the colonies in the hope of making a better life for themselves and their families.

What awaited these newcomers was not merely a single New World but a variety of colonies. Having been founded for different reasons and settled by various groups of immigrants, the thirteen colonies had, by the mid–eighteenth century, developed distinct characteristics. The character of each colony—along with environmental factors such as climate and soil conditions—influenced the way of life of its inhabitants.

The Northeastern Colonies

Massachusetts, New Hampshire, Rhode Island, and Connecticut were established as settlements. These colonies were founded by immigrants determined to build communities where their families could live according to strongly held religious principles. (Maine had been an-nexed by Massachusetts in 1651 and was not governed as a separate colony. Vermont separated from New Hampshire only in 1777, becoming the fourteenth state.) Best known of the immigrant groups to this area are the Pilgrims, who landed in 1620 and established Plymouth Plantation. The Pilgrims were followed by groups of Puritans, who, by the end of 1630, had established Boston and ten other towns in Massachusetts.

Convinced that God was about to punish the Anglican Church in England for its corruption, the Puritans came to America to escape this sign of divine retribution and to establish a way of life that accorded with their beliefs. Francis Higginson, an early Puritan, explained the foundation of these convictions in his book *New-Englands Plantation*:

> That which is our greatest comfort, and means of defence above all others, is, that we have here the true Religion and holy Ordinances of Almightie God taught among us . . . thus we doubt not but God will be with us, and if God be with us, who can be against us?[7]

The Puritans worshiped in a simple style, rejecting the vestments (elaborate gowns worn by Anglican priests) and altar cloths that they disapprovingly associated with Catholic forms of worship. Moreover, they allowed only accepted church members who had demonstrated their faith to participate in governing their towns and cities. However, disagreements arose amongst the faith-inspired people who were New England's first colonists. As a result, some groups split away to form new settlements, such as Providence, Rhode Island, and the towns of the Connecticut River valley.

Close-Knit New England Towns

New England towns were built with houses close together around a church and village green, and the surrounding farmland and pasturage was carefully divided among the town's families. By 1750 religious life in New England was no longer as intense as it had been in the seventeenth century, and the tight social controls of earlier times had loosened. However, the communities still tended to be close-knit, and the tradition of involvement by most white men in the running of town affairs continued. This approach was very different from the way that public affairs were conducted in England, where only the wealthy and members of the nobility could exercise political power.

Boston, with a population of about 16,000, was the largest city in the northeastern colonies. Massachusetts also had two other important seaports, Salem and Marblehead, each with more than 3,000 inhabitants. The other major population centers of New England were Portsmouth, New Hampshire; Newburyport, Massachusetts; Providence, Rhode Island; and New Haven and Hartford, Connecticut. About 85 percent of the population in the northeastern colonies was engaged in farming, but crafts and cottage industries were growing in significance, and commerce was also important. Boston mer-

A group of New England Puritans walks to church. The Puritans worshiped in a simple style and allowed only those who could demonstrate their faith to govern them.

Boston was the largest city in the northeastern colonies. Merchant ships used its port for trading, fishing, and whaling.

chants pursued trade with the West Indies and Europe, calling at other colonial ports to buy goods for export. Fishing and whaling provided the livelihoods of many New Englanders, while others supported their families by cutting timber to sell abroad.

The Middle Colonies

New York, Delaware, and New Jersey, settled by the Dutch and people from fourteen other European ethnic groups, were intended in their early years to be profit-making colonies rather than religious communities. Dutch settlement of the New World began in 1624, and in 1626 Dutch colonists bought the island of Manhattan from its native inhabitants for the sum of sixty guilders. In New York, then called New Amsterdam, the Dutch originally assigned large holdings of land, called patroonships, to a few individuals. These patroons developed fur trading for export to Europe but did little to promote the settlement of villages and farms. After many governmental conflicts and wars with powerful Indian nations, New York and Delaware were taken over by the English. By 1750, however, these areas were still less densely settled than the land along the New England coast.

By 1760 the city of New York had overtaken Boston in size with eighteen thousand inhabitants, still considerably fewer than those who lived in rapidly growing Philadelphia. Albany was the only other town of any size in the colony of New York. The New

Jersey townships of Elizabeth and Newark were still small.

Quaker Settlements

New Jersey became a place of refuge for Quakers, and many Puritans also settled there. However, this colony had a proprietor, essentially an owner, and for this reason William Penn, a wealthy English Quaker, thought it was not completely secure from religious persecution. Penn determined to create a colony of his own.

In 1681 King Charles II repaid a large debt that he owed to William Penn by making him the proprietor of an extensive territory, which was named Pennsylvania. In accordance with Penn's religious beliefs, he welcomed settlers of all Christian faiths to live in what he called a "holy experiment." The land and climate here were very good for farming, unlike the rocky soil and cold winters of New England, and the Delaware River formed an excellent harbor. The city of Philadelphia arose here, and by 1760 it was the largest city in the colonies with a population of twenty-three thousand.

Pennsylvania farmers often grew wheat, a crop that was valued because it produced a finer flour than the Indian corn grown in New England, and it therefore made a better quality of bread. Farms that were located along a navigable river, such as the Delaware River or New York's Hudson River, were able to sell their produce profitably in the growing cities and even to export wheat and flour.

Conflicts Between English and German Settlers

In the first half of the eighteenth century, large numbers of German-speaking immigrants—possibly as many as a hundred thousand—arrived in the American colonies, especially Pennsylvania and New York. By 1760 one-third of the inhabitants of Pennsylvania were of German origin. Some of the English-

A Bought Servant

In his *Autobiography*, reprinted in editor George McMichael's *Anthology of American Literature*, Ben Franklin described the men who worked with him in a printing house in Philadelphia. Of his four coworkers, two were indentured servants. One of these servants was very unusual because he had a college education.

"It was an odd Thing to find an Oxford Scholar in the Situation of a bought Servant. He was not more than 18 Years of Age, and gave me this Account of himself; that he was born in Gloucester, educated at a Grammar School there, had been distinguish'd among the Scholars for some apparent Superiority in performing his Part when they exhibited Plays. . . . Thence he was sent to Oxford; there he continu'd about a Year, but not well satisfy'd, wishing of all things to see London and become a Player [actor]. At length receiving his Quarterly Allowance . . . he walk'd out of Town, hid his [academic] Gown in a Bush, and footed it to London, where having no Friend to advise him, he fell into bad Company, soon spent his Guineas [English coins], . . . grew necessitous, pawn'd his Cloaths and wanted Bread. Walking the Street very hungry, and not knowing what to do with himself, a Crimp's Bill [an advertisement enticing people into indentures] was put into his Hand, offering immediate. . . . Encouragement to such as would bind themselves to serve in America."

A typical farm located in Germantown, Pennsylvania. Many German immigrants seeking a new life in the colonies settled in Pennsylvania.

speaking colonists worried that their language and way of life would disappear from the New World. Pennsylvania lawmakers even considered preventing anyone who did not speak English from holding a government position.

Benjamin Franklin, reflecting the English prejudice against Germans, was concerned that these immigrants kept themselves apart from the other colonists by socializing in their own taverns, worshiping in their own churches, and even drinking coffee rather than tea. Franklin complained, "Why should the [German] boors be suffered to swarm into our settlements, and by hearding [herding] together, establish their language and manners, to the exclusion of ours?"[8]

Franklin's fears and prejudices were misguided, and later in life he came to regret them. These fears were also groundless because the English way of life—especially the language and legal system—was soon predominant throughout the colonies.

Settlement in the South followed quite a different pattern from the lifestyle developed by immigrants whose major purpose was to establish a new community or to trade for furs. In contrast, the southern colonists' goal was to create plantations that would allow them to grow crops for export to Europe.

Jamestown, Virginia, was the site of the first permanent English colony in the New World. Though this settlement almost failed in its first years, the leaders of the Virginia Company, who were authorized to colonize the region, continued to search for a way to realize some profit from their enterprise. In 1612 colonist John Rolfe introduced sweet West Indian tobacco to Virginia, and the colonists found a crop with an eager market in England.

The Culture of Tobacco

The fact that tobacco was the major crop in this region had a strong effect on the way the colonists lived. Tobacco quickly depleted the soil, so it could only be grown in a given field for a few years. For this reason, a tobacco planter had to own large amounts of land for crop rotation. He also needed river frontage

Ships carrying tobacco move along the James River to their eventual trading destinations. Tobacco proved to be a profitable crop for southern colonists.

so that the heavy barrels of tobacco could be rolled onto a wharf and loaded onboard a ship. As a result, rather than tightly settled New England–style villages or mid-Atlantic cities, the people of the tobacco-growing areas created far-flung plantations along waterways. The planters developed a sense of independence and enterprise as they carved new fields out of the wilderness, managed their households and workers, and sold their cash crops on the international market.

By the early eighteenth century, Virginia's tidewater plantations were well established, with an average size of five thousand acres. Although they were a minority of the colonists, the landowners of these large estates held most of the wealth and power. Their position depended, first, on the labor of indentured servants from Europe and, later, on the work of slaves from Africa.

A Refuge for Catholics

Maryland was also a plantation state. With its many rivers and estuaries along Chesapeake Bay, Maryland offered easy access to shipping and to European markets. Originally established as a refuge for English Catholics, Maryland was strongly influenced by the aristocratic ideals of its proprietors, who planned for large landholdings by a few wealthy planters. By the mid–eighteenth century this ideal had broken down, but Maryland's colonists still lived on sprawling farms.

As was true in Virginia, there were few towns in Maryland; even the capital city, Annapolis, was very small. In 1750 Virginia's capital, Williamsburg, had only two hundred houses and about one thousand inhabitants, not including those who arrived for a session of the legislature, the House of Burgesses. Annapolis was even smaller. An English visitor, Andrew Burnaby, wrote a book about his travels in the colonies and described Annapolis: "None of the streets are paved, and the few public buildings here are not worth mentioning. The church is a very poor one, the stadt-house [state house] but indifferent, and the governor's palace is not finished."[9] At this time, life in Virginia and Maryland centered around the plantation, not the city.

Albemarle, Clarendon, and Georgia

The Carolinas began as a single colony divided into two provinces, Albemarle and Clarendon. The earliest proprietors had formerly owned small sugar plantations in Barbados but had been elbowed out by larger planters. Instead, they hoped to make their fortune in the Carolinas and planned to recruit settlers from Barbados and New England. However, the first settlers were more attracted to fur trading than to farming.

Albemarle—which would later become North Carolina—was settled in large part by people who moved there from Virginia and other colonies. In general, North Carolina settlers practiced subsistence farming, raising food for the support of their own families. They sometimes also grew a small amount of tobacco and corn that they could

Traveling Between the Colonies

The colonies were separated by more than cultural differences, and the untamed landscape made travel dangerous. In 1704 Sarah Kemble Knight, a thirty-eight-year-old widow, made the difficult journey on horseback from Boston to New Haven and then on to New York. In her journal, reprinted in editor William L. Andrews's *Journeys in New Worlds: Early American Women's Narratives*, Knight described the experience of being taken by canoe across a swollen river between Connecticut and Massachusetts.

"The next day wee come to a river which by Reason of the Freshetts coming down was swell'd so high wee feared it impassable and the rapid stream was very terryfying—However we must over and that in a small Cannoo. Mr. Rogers assuring me of his good Conduct, I after a stay of near an howr on the shore for consultation went into the Cannoo, and Mr. Rogers paddled about 100 yards up the Creek by the shore side, turned into the swift strem and dexterously steering her in a moment wee come to the other side as swiftly passing as an arrow shott out of the Bow by a strong arm. I staid on the shore till hee returned to fetch our horses, which he caused to swim over himself bringing the furniture [i.e., harnesses] in the Cannoo. But it is past my skill to express the Exceeding fright all their transactions formed in me."

sell to New England traders. The region had no towns and few churches.

The economy of Clarendon (or South Carolina) focused on the production of cash crops, and these were likely to be grown on large plantations that relied on slave labor. The way of life in South Carolina was strongly influenced by the English immigrants who had come there from sugar plantations in Barbados. With them they brought commercial attitudes toward farming and familiarity with the use of slaves. A relatively small group of white planters in South Carolina became enormously wealthy raising rice, indigo, and tobacco. These planters often made extended visits to the gracious city of Charleston, which reflected their wealth and their desire for elegance and luxury.

Georgia was established in the 1730s as a charitable solution to the problems of crime and poverty in England. The colony's founders planned to help the poor of London by providing them with small farms where they could redeem their lives through hard work and provide the region's Native Americans with an example of Christian living. Originally both slavery and alcoholic beverages were prohibited in Georgia.

The trustees of Georgia raised subscriptions from people across England to pay for the colony and to send England's unfortunates to this new country, which the founders had never seen. To avoid the discrepancies of wealth that had arisen in other southern colonies, they restricted landholdings to a maximum of five hundred acres. Unlike the founders of other colonies, the Georgia trustees did not set up an assembly but instead governed the colony themselves.

The founders of Georgia believed that they knew enough to plan farms and have their settlers cultivate profitable crops. Yet most of the settlers had spent their lives in the streets and jails of London, and they had no knowledge of agricultural practices or experience with heavy manual labor. The land and climate also proved unsuitable for the kinds of agriculture that the trustees had planned. Af-ter the collapse of the founders' well-intentioned but impractical scheme, the people of the colony took many years to build up the governmental skills and independent attitudes that prevailed in Virginia, Massachusetts, and the other colonies. Only five thousand settlers were living in Georgia in 1750.

Slavery in the Colonies

Slavery began in the Americas when Portuguese planters took Africans by force and used them as farm laborers on huge plantations in South and Central America. English planters in the Caribbean exploited slave labor in the cultivation of sugar, and the practice of owning and using slaves was later introduced to North America. The type of agriculture carried out in the southern colonies was highly labor-intensive, and it was very difficult for the planters to hire enough free men and women to do this work. Captives brought to the New World from Africa fulfilled this enormous need. By the first quarter of the eighteenth century, the economy of the southern colonies was dependent on slave labor.

Most of the Africans who came to the Americas were from the interior of West Africa and were taken captive by a coastal nation during a war. Slavery was a traditional African practice; starting in the seventeenth century, however, those who took captives found a new and lucrative market amongst the colonists of the New World. African slave traders marched their captives—often in groups tied together by ropes around their hands and necks—to the coast, where they were sold to European traders and loaded onboard ships.

Conditions during the voyage to America were appalling. Slaves were crowded closely into dark spaces below deck, with nothing more than an open tub as a toilet. In good

African slaves work on a cotton plantation in the American South. The southern colonies became dependent on slave labor during the eighteenth century.

weather they might be taken on deck for forced exercise, but in bad weather—or when the crew feared that their human cargo might rebel—they were chained permanently below deck. Disease flourished in these conditions, and traders expected many deaths among the slaves. Those who survived the journey had to face the indignity of being sold. In the colonies (unlike the custom in Africa itself), slaves had no legal status as humans and were considered the personal property of their owners.

The Slave Population

The slave population of the thirteen colonies grew rapidly. During the mid–eighteenth century, the largest group of people to come to the colonies was captives from Africa. In 1700 blacks, virtually all of whom were slaves, comprised about 11 percent of the colonial population. By 1770 this proportion

had doubled to 22 percent, the highest level in American history. Shortly before the American Revolution, 460,000 slaves were living in the colonies, mostly in the South. Sixty percent of the inhabitants of South Carolina were slaves, but the proportion was far smaller in the northern colonies. For example, in Pennsylvania slaves comprised only 2 percent of the population.

In the mid–eighteenth century, the majority of the slave population—60 percent—worked on the tobacco plantations of Maryland and Virginia. A further 30 percent lived and worked in North Carolina, South Carolina, and Georgia. The remaining 10 percent of the slave population lived in northern states, particularly in the cities of New York, Boston, and Providence.

Being a slave in the New World made heavy demands on these unwilling immigrants. Cut off from everything they knew, the colonial slaves had to learn a new language and new ways to work. Forming relationships with slaves who had come earlier or who were born

Thoughts on Slavery

Having emigrated from France, Michel-Guillaume-Jean de Crèvecoeur was very proud of his new country. When he traveled from his farm in New York to visit Charleston, however, he was filled with horror as he saw how the slaves were treated. Crèvecoeur's essay about slavery, "Descriptions of Charleston; Thoughts on Slavery; on Physical Evil; a Melancholy Scene," is letter IX in his book *Letters from an American Farmer*, excerpted in editor George McMichael's *Anthology of American Literature*.

"While all is joy, festivity, and happiness in Charleston, would you imagine that scenes of misery overspread in the country? Their ears by habit are become deaf; their hearts are hardened; they neither see, hear, nor feel for the woes of their poor slaves from whose painful labors all their wealth proceeds. Here the horrors of slavery, the hardship of incessant toils, are unseen, and no one thinks with compassion of those showers of sweat and of tears which from the bodies of Africans daily drop and moisten the ground they till. The cracks of the whip urging these miserable begins to excessive labour are far too distant from the gay capital to be heard. The chosen race eat, drink, and live happy, while the unfortunate one grubs up the ground, raises indigo, or husks the rice, exposed to a sun full as scorching as their native one, without the support of good food, without the cordials of any cheering liquor.

This great contrast has often afforded me subjects of the most afflicting meditation. On the one side, behold a people enjoying all that life affords most bewitching and pleasurable, without labour, without fatigue, hardly subjected to the trouble of wishing. With gold . . . they order vessels to the coasts of Guinea [West Africa]; by virtue of that gold, wars, murders, and devastations are committed in some harmless, peaceable African neighborhood where dwelt innocent people who even knew not but that all men were black. The daughter torn from her weeping mother, the child from the wretched parents, the wife from the loving husband, whole families swept away and brought through storms and tempests to this rich metropolis! There, arranged like horses at a fair, they are branded like cattle and then driven to toil, to starve, and to languish for a few years on the different plantations of these citizens."

in the New World was sometimes difficult, and so were the demands by whites that blacks adopt a "racial etiquette" acknowledging the right of all whites to dominate all blacks. While it is clear that thousands of Africans survived and provided the labor for which they had been bought, many found ways to undermine the system. A traveler to the South described the resistance he observed among new slaves in harsh but respectful terms:

A new negro if he must be broke, either from obstinacy, or, which I am more apt to suppose, from greatness of soul, will require more hard discipline than a young spaniel. You would be surprised at their perseverance; let a hundred men show him how to hoe, or drive a wheelbarrow, he'll still take [pick up] the one by the bottom and the other by the wheel; and they often die before they can be conquered.[10]

24 Life in the American Colonies

Slaves worked as domestic servants and sometimes as skilled craftsmen in cities as well as on plantations. Other slaves worked alongside their owners on small farms that had only one or two Africans. Most slaves, however, labored fifteen-hour days on southern tobacco or rice plantations. Under these terrible conditions, hundreds of thousands of African Americans took their place in the life of the New World.

The immigrants who came to the New World in the eighteenth century found many different worlds, depending on the conditions of their arrival and where they settled. Some were determined to create for themselves a new religious world, while others came to make their fortunes. Many colonists had chosen to immigrate, but large numbers of others were brought here against their will. The cold winters of the North shaped the lives of the New England colonists, while the climate of the South meant that the cultivation of crops like tobacco and indigo determined the pace of life. Even within each colony, life in the city was a different world from life in the countryside.

Living in a Colonial City

Originally the cities and towns of colonial America reflected the culture of the Europeans who built them. Many American communities, like Boston and New York, were named for places in the colonists' country of origin. Other cities, like Charleston and Williamsburg, were named in honor of British monarchs. Yet some names show the beginning of something new: a distinctly American way of life based on heartfelt ideals. The founders of Philadelphia, for instance, were expressing their intention to establish a loving and open community when they chose a name meaning "brotherly love" in Greek. Place names like Providence, New Haven, Salem, and New Canaan illustrate the religious and biblical values of their original settlers.

Even in the New World, though, colonial citizens lived much as they would have in a European city, with similar class distinctions and forms of craft and industry. Although the New World communities were relatively small, there were still gaps in income and social standing between the social classes. There were no dukes, earls, or counts, but a few wealthy families lived much more luxurious lives even than the successful merchants. The craftsmen and artisans of the cities had more respect and a more comfortable way of life than unskilled laborers. The poor often lived in shacks and lacked decent clothing and adequate food, just as was true in the Old World. Yet many immigrants of all social classes found opportunities in the New World that would not have been available to them in the rigid society of a European city.

At the start of the eighteenth century, Boston was the only American city of any size. New York, Philadelphia, and Charleston were little more than villages. However, immigration led to the rapid growth of these cities. By 1760 Philadelphia had approximately twenty-three thousand inhabitants and was soon to become one of the largest cities in the British Empire. New York, with about eighteen thousand inhabitants, had surpassed Boston, which had a population in the vicinity of sixteen thousand. In the mid–eighteenth century, the only city of any size in the South was Charleston, which had about eight thousand residents.

The Location and Layout of Cities

Since the colonial settlers came by sea, most of their cities were on the coast and were used as secure locations from which the surrounding countryside could be explored and colonized. Boston, for example, was the administrative center of the Massachusetts Bay Company. The Dutch colonists who founded New Amsterdam administered from the city the patroonship system that controlled the countryside. By the mid–eighteenth century, some of these ports had become significant trading centers as well as places of arrival for thousands of new immigrants.

Most of the cities of Europe had grown up slowly. Some began as crossing points on rivers; others evolved from medieval ports or trading locations. The gradual growth of these towns usually meant that they developed haphazardly, with no underlying plan and with narrow, twisting streets. In contrast, the European settlers of North America were able to plan their new communities. For this reason, many colonial towns and cities were built systematically, with streets laid out in a grid. Boston was an exception, but most colonial cities had an orderly layout.

The designers of New Haven, for example, envisioned a city of symmetrical perfection. They built it in a square divided by a grid of streets into nine smaller squares. The central square—called the "Green"—was common land, and at its center stood a meet-inghouse that was itself a perfect square. William Penn's design for Philadelphia was also a grid, but he used rectangles instead. Two major streets divided the city into quarters and formed a central meeting square.

City Streets

Although the gridwork layout of a colonial city may look neat and orderly on a map, the actual streets were usually dirty and difficult to travel on. Since the streets were unpaved, the wheels of carts and coaches made deep ruts. Rain and snow sometimes made it impossible for horses to pull vehicles through the mud. A further problem was the lack of sewers. City dwellers, with no plumbing, threw their waste out onto the street, where

The settlers of North America planned out their cities and built them systematically. This map shows a section of New York in 1767.

it smelled bad and often contaminated the wells used for drinking water.

Boston was the first colonial city to address these problems. In 1690 the city authorities improved the drainage of the streets and paved them with cobblestones, which are rounded stones that are closely packed together to form a durable surface. Fourteen years later Francis Thresher, a private citizen, built the first city sewer in Boston, and others soon followed his example.

Public Buildings

In New England towns and cities the most important public buildings—and the first to be built—were usually places of worship. By the 1700s, these towns often had several churches and meetinghouses, reflecting both the religious divisions that had arisen among the descendants of the earliest settlers and the diversity of the continuing flow of immigrants. Joseph Bennett, an Englishman who visited Boston in the summer of 1740, wrote a description of the city's places of worship. Accustomed to seeing only one Anglican church in each village at home, Bennett was surprised by the large number in the small town of Boston:

> There are three Episcopal churches, one of which is called the King's Chapel, and has a handsome organ, and a magnificent seat for the Governor, who goes to this place when [a member] of the Church of England; and there are nine Independent meeting-houses, one Anabaptist meeting, one Quakers' meeting, and one French Church.[11]

The democratic nature of New England's settlements created a need for public buildings where people could gather to debate issues and carry out the functions of local government. In Boston Peter Faneuil donated the building known as Faneuil Hall to the city in 1742 as a public meeting place. In Philadelphia, Pennsylvania's State House, which would later be known as Independence Hall, was completed in 1741. Williamsburg, the administrative center

New York City Drivers

During her visit to New York City in 1704, Sarah Kemble Knight was taken on a trip out of town, where she was impressed by the hospitality of New Yorkers. However, like many recent visitors to New York, she was appalled by the driving she saw there. Her journal has been reprinted in editor William L. Andrews's *Journeys in New Worlds: Early American Women's Narratives.*

"Their Diversions in the Winter is Riding Sleighs about three or four Miles out of Town, where they have Houses of entertainment at a place called the Bowery, and some go to friends Houses who handsomely [i.e., generously] treat them. Mr. Burroughs cary'd his spouse and Daughter and myself out to one Madame Dowes, a Gentlewoman that lived at a farm House, who gave us a handsome Entertainment of five or six Dishes and choice Beer and metheglin [i.e., mead], Cyder, etc. all which she said was the produce of her farm. I believe we mett 50 or 60 sleighs that day—they fly with great swiftness and some are so furious that they'le turn out of the path for none except a Loaden Cart. Nor do they spare for any diversion the place affords, and sociable to a degree, they'r Tables being as free to their Naybours as to themselves."

Donated to Boston in 1742, Faneuil Hall served as a public meeting place for residents of the large city.

for the Virginia colony, had its Governor's Palace, completed in 1720. The Colony House in Newport, Rhode Island, was finished in 1739.

The men who used these government buildings for political debate often continued their discussions in nearby taverns. These were busy places where people ate, drank, and sometimes negotiated business deals. It was in a Philadelphia tavern that the teenaged Ben Franklin met with the governor of Pennsylvania to discuss his printing business. As Franklin recorded in his *Autobiography*, "Over the Madeira [wine] he propos'd my Setting up my Business [and] laid before me the probabilities of Success." [12]

Commerce in the Cities

Along with the population growth of North America's towns and cities during the eighteenth century came economic development. Formerly, these towns and cities had been primarily trading locations, where farm produce and raw materials from the surrounding countryside were exported and manufactured goods from overseas were imported. However, as the colonial economy developed, new industries began to emerge. While milling and iron making had to be carried out near the sources of power (water and firewood), materials like timber, iron bars, and even flour were increasingly made into finished goods in city workshops.

The northern colonies were strongly influenced by their trade with the West Indies. The planters of the West Indies had specialized in the production of sugar and were no longer self-sufficient in other staples. This specialization provided a ready market to the colonists of North America. They exported large quantities of flour and pickled meat, and trading ships returned to North America with cargoes of sugar and molasses, which were distilled into rum.

The Effects of Business Success

The rapid growth of Philadelphia illustrates the effect of the expanding colonial economy during the mid–eighteenth century. The city experienced great changes in its way of life as non-Quakers moved there and began to develop successful businesses. Planned by the Quaker William Penn, Philadelphia grew rapidly into a center of trade. By the 1750s many other groups had added their numbers to this community, and the city reflected their cultures and the success of their business ventures. Philadelphia had become the market for produce from the inland farms. As one settler said, "Our lands have been grateful to us and have begun to reward our labors with abounding crops of corn." [13] Philadelphia merchants made fortunes shipping this corn, as well as wheat, barley, rye, biscuits, fruits, and meat, to Massachusetts,

Rhode Island, and New York. Their ships also sailed to the islands of the Caribbean and to Ireland, England, and Spain.

In Charleston both merchants and planters were important in guiding city affairs. Most wealthy planters fled the rice-growing areas and lived in the city during the times when disease-bearing insects filled the marshlands. Charleston residents enjoyed a lively social life, which included dancing and going to plays, races, and concerts. They imported luxury items from the Old World, including clothing, cloth, shoes, gloves, hats, silverware, furniture, and medicine. To pay for these expensive imported goods, they exported their abundant crops.

Busy Seaports

Exports of another kind were important to the economy of the New England colonies. Fishing boats returning from the great fishing banks of Maine and Newfoundland would come into the ports of New England. The catch was usually dried or pickled with salt and packed into barrels before being shipped to Europe, where many Catholics

The settlement of New Amsterdam served as a successful trade port for merchant ships. Many northern colonies became centers of trade during the mid–eighteenth century.

ate fish on the days that the Church forbade them to eat meat. Poor-quality fish was exported to the West Indies to feed the slaves.

Whaling provided a wide range of goods for use by colonial people as well as for export. This form of commerce depended on ships sailing from most New England and eastern Long Island ports. Whale oil was burned in lamps and provided a valuable source of light that was cleaner and brighter than candles. Many families ate whale meat, and women used narrow strips of whalebone to stiffen their corsets. Perfume was made from ambergris, a strong-smelling material sometimes found in whale intestines.

As all of these industries prospered, the colonial ports became increasingly busy. Shipbuilding rose in importance, and thousands of seamen worked on the ships while many other workers prepared and packed goods for shipping and operated warehouses. Middlemen found opportunities in the distribution of products, and clerks were employed in accounting. Insurance was increasingly used, and countinghouses—the predecessors of banks—emerged.

City Building Styles

By building in a style that was fashionable in a European city, wealthy citizens of the colonies demonstrated that they were up-to-date with fashion and that their cities were vibrant centers of commerce and culture. Boston, for example, maintained strong links with London, and many of its buildings showed the influence of English style. Boston's churches had originally been built in a plain style with a simple belfry. However, as travelers returned from London in the mid–eighteenth century, they introduced the new English style of a church with a steeple. The houses of the very

wealthy in Boston resembled the mansions of the English nobility.

In the 1700s New York's architecture reflected its origins as a Dutch colony and its continuing links with the Netherlands. In her journal, Sarah Kemble Knight, who traveled to New York in 1704, wrote a description of the buildings she saw. Coming from the British-influenced—and at that time much larger—city of Boston, she was struck by the unfamiliar style of architecture of New York houses:

> The Cittie of New York is a pleasant, well compacted place, situated on a Commodius River which is a fine harbour for shipping. The Buildings Brick Generaly, very stately and high, though not altogether like ours in Boston. The Bricks in some of the Houses are of divers [various] Coullers [colors] and laid in Checkers, being glazed look very agreeable. The inside of them are neat to admiration, the wooden work (for only the walls are plasterd) and the Sumers [beams] and Joists are plained and kept very white scowr'd, and so are all the partitions if made of Bords. . . . The hearths were laid with the finest tile that I ever see, and the stair cases laid all with white tile which is ever clean, and so are the walls of the Kitchen which had a brick floor.[14]

Built by the Dutch as New Amsterdam, New York originally looked like a city in Holland. Wooden, brick, or stone houses had curved gables or stepped roof ends. Houses tended to be long and narrow, with the narrow end facing the street, just as houses in Amsterdam faced the canals of that city. The gable ends, which could be seen by passersby, were decorated with colored tiles and carved woodwork. English styles gradually took over

The houses of New York were originally modeled after Dutch homes. English-style homes did not become popular in this city until 1765.

in New York, and in 1765 a building company advertised houses in the *New York Mercury* "built after the London taste."[15] The great fire of 1776 wiped out whole streets of Dutch houses from the New York cityscape. The homes that replaced them were largely built in the English style.

The Diverse Heritage of Charleston's Buildings

As Charleston, South Carolina, developed in the mid–eighteenth century, the city lacked a unified architectural heritage. Thus, Charleston drew on the diversity of attitudes, skills, and beliefs brought by the English, the immigrants from the West Indies, and peoples from many European cultures. All these groups had different customs, traditions, arts, and languages.

From West Indian architectural styles Charleston received its stucco houses, which often had iron balconies and multilevel piazzas. The tile roofs of these dwellings were modeled after houses in Jamaica and Barbados. Some Charleston houses had gables like those of New York or Old Amsterdam, and some roofs had pantiles in the style of southern

Fire Fighting in Colonial Cities

Fire was a serious hazard. In the seventeenth century Boston suffered a number of serious fires that spread from house to house. In 1691 the city purchased a fire engine equipped with buckets and hand pumps and decreed that all new buildings were to be made of brick.

Benjamin Franklin was concerned about the risk of fires in Philadelphia. In 1735 he published an article "on the different Accidents and Carelessnesses by which Houses were set on fire, with Cautions against them, and Means proposed of avoiding them." He explains in his *Autobiography*, found in George McMichael's *Anthology of American Literature*, how his suggestions were taken up and resulted in the formation of a fire company "for the more ready Extinguishing of Fires, and mutual Assistance in Removing and Securing of Goods when in Danger."

"Associates in this Scheme were presently found amounting to Thirty. Our Articles of Agreement oblig'd every Member to keep always in good Order and fit for Use, a certain Number of Leather Buckets, with strong Bags and Baskets (for packing and transporting of Goods) which were to be brought to every Fire; and we agreed to meet once a Month and spend a social Evening together, in discoursing and communicating such Ideas as occur'd to us upon the Subject of Fires as might be useful in our Conduct on such Occasions."

The fire company was successful, and soon other companies were formed. Franklin proudly describes how far Philadelphia's fire fighting has come in the fifty years since that first company was formed.

"The small Fines that have been paid by Members for Absence at the Monthly Meetings, have been apply'd to the Purchase of Fire Engines, Ladders, Firehooks, and other useful Implements for each Company, so that I question whether there is a City in the World better provided with the Means of putting a Stop to beginning Conflagrations."

An early fire engine douses a fire in New York.

France. Wealthy English immigrants to Charleston built Georgian mansions like those of their homeland. Painted pink, green, yellow, or blue, the stucco exteriors of the Charleston houses added a beautiful air of distinction to the streets of the city. The home of one wealthy citizen, Miles Brewton, had a porch with Ionic capitals on its columns, lively carved cornices, marble mantelpieces, and spacious, graceful rooms.

The Lives of Wealthy City Dwellers

The wealthy people in colonial cities had relatively comfortable lives. Although their homes did not have bathrooms or running water, servants carried hot water for washing to the family bedrooms. The servants would also serve meals and clean up afterwards, while the employer concerned himself with business and social affairs and often was active in government. The employer's wife was generally responsible for the household affairs, including planning meals and entertainment and managing the servants.

Rich city dwellers could afford horses and carriages that not only helped them get from place to place but also reflected their wealth and status in society. Upper-class people also demonstrated their wealth by filling their houses with possessions. They ate with silver forks and spoons and used teapots made by silversmiths like Paul Revere. They also hung expensive artworks on the walls of their homes. To have their portraits painted, they employed an artist such as John Singleton Copley, whose portraits are among the best-known American works of art.

While the wealthy lived in mansions constructed of brick or stone, craftsmen and laborers lived in smaller houses made of wood. Typically these homes had two rooms downstairs, two bedrooms upstairs, and a lean-to kitchen at the rear. Although they were not farmers, many city families also had a shed where they kept chickens and a pig or a cow to provide the family with eggs, meat, and milk.

Public Education

Aware that their prosperity depended on their reading and writing skills and their knowledge of accounting and law, wealthy city dwellers sent their sons to schools where skills like these were taught. Many children

Located in Boston, the Hancock Mansion belonged to a wealthy colonial family. The wealthy usually played leading roles in society and enjoyed many privileges.

were sent to private tutors and academies. In some cities, however, education was also available to the public. Boston, for example, had five public schools, where the only charge was firewood to help heat the school. These public schools offered boys from the middle class the opportunity to learn skills that could lead to greater prosperity.

In New York, Dutch colonists were still a majority of the population, but many children went to English schools so that they would avoid the embarrassment of speaking broken English. One schoolmaster, John Lewis, advertised that his students were instructed in "speaking, reading, spelling and writing English." He also taught arithmetic, navigation, geometry, and trigonometry, as well as the "elements of geography and astronomy, with several other useful branches of the mathematics and literature." [16]

Some of the schools in Charleston reflected the educational ideas of the English upper classes by teaching Latin and Greek grammar and composition. The boys read Ovid, Virgil, Tacitus, Homer, and Euripides. Upper-class girls learned dancing, music, embroidery, drawing, needlework, and French. Another Charleston schoolmaster,

"A Minuet with Miss Soley"

Anna Green Winslow was a young colonial girl who moved with her wealthy parents from Boston to Nova Scotia. When Anna was eleven, they sent her back to live with her aunt so that she could go to school and learn the social graces (including handwriting and dancing) appropriate for an upper-class girl. Anna had received special permission to attend a party, which was for girls only, although some of the parents also attended as "spectators." The girls danced and also played games like "wooing a widow." Anna described the party, which she calls a "constitation," in her journal, which she wrote in the form of letters to her parents. Her journal has since been reprinted as the *Diary of Anna Green Winslow*.

"January 17, 1771. I told you on the 27th that I was going to a constitation with miss Soley. I have now the pleasure to give you the result, viz. a very genteel well regulated assembly which we had at Mr Soley's last evening, miss Soley being mistress of the ceremony. Mrs. Soley desired me to assist Miss Hannah in making out a list of guests which I did some time since, I wrote all the invitation cards. There was a large company assembled in a handsome, large, upper room in the new end of the house. We had two fiddles, & I had the honor to open the diversion of the evening in a minuet with miss Soley. . . .

Our treat was nuts, raisins, Cakes, Wine, punch, hot & cold, all in great plenty. We had a very agreeable evening from 5 to 10 o'clock. For variety we woo'd a widow, hunted the whistle, threaded the needle, & while the company was collecting, we diverted ourselves with playing of pawns, no rudeness Mamma I assure you. . . .

I was dressed in my yellow coat, black bib and apron, black feathers on my head, my past [paste, or costume jewelry] comb, & all my past garnet marquesett & jet pins, together with my silver plume—my loket [locket], rings, black collar round my neck, black mitts [net gloves] & 2 or 3 yards of blue ribbin, (black and blue is high taste) striped tucker and ruffels (not my best) & my silk shoes completed my dress."

William Walton, believed that boys who would grow up to be merchants or planters should have a more practical education. His curriculum included English, arithmetic, bookkeeping, geography, and history. At a nearby school the students could learn algebra, geometry, surveying, navigation, and astronomy.

The Arts in the Colonial City

Boston had a number of bookshops selling literature in Latin and Greek as well as books about philosophy, astronomy, divinity, medicine, law, and government. Perhaps because of Boston's Puritan roots, these bookstores did not sell many contemporary novels. As one critic wrote at the time,

> Among all the licentious follies which corrupt the mind there is not one which has done more hurt in the present age than the vast quantity of idle and immoral books. A simple amusement in reading is such a ridiculous trifling away of time that any person of common sense must on the least reflection condemn themselves. [17]

In 1756 John Mein started the first public library, where readers who paid an annual subscription could borrow books. Writing about his new enterprise, Mein said, "Something of this kind has been long wanted, to amuse the man of leisure, to afford an elegant and agreeable relaxation to the minds of men of business and to insinuate knowledge and instruction under the veil of entertainment to the fair sex." [18]

In addition to novels, many religious groups objected strongly to theater, thinking that it would have a corrupting effect on society. Consequently, theater was almost unheard-

Benjamin Franklin arranged the opening of the first subscription library in Philadelphia. These public libraries became more popular after 1765.

of in Boston. In New York, however, groups of actors were able to put on plays in empty warehouses, and by 1735 there was a "play house" on Broadway. These early theaters had raised stages that were lit by candles, while a simple chandelier hung above the audience. They presented plays by Shakespeare and by contemporary British playwrights.

Centers of Colonial Thought

These cities, so different in character, were separated by days of difficult traveling. As seaports, however, they had regular commercial and cultural contact with Europe and the West Indies. Though small by today's standards, Boston, New York, Philadelphia, Charleston, and Williamsburg were centers of colonial life and thought. They were also the areas most directly affected when the English government imposed more and more restrictive taxes on the colonial economy.

Most colonials were surprised by the difficulties they began to encounter during this period. The British had conquered Montreal in 1760, ending the wars with France that had threatened peace and stability in North America. In addition, colonial people were proud of their rights as Englishmen, yet the distance from the seat of government caused increasing problems. After the end of the French and Indian War, the British government had enormous territories to govern and defend, and they needed the revenues to pay for their operations in America. In 1764 Parliament passed the Currency Act and the Sugar Act, which imposed high taxes on the colonies.

As a result, the tide of political opinion in the colonies began to turn against acceptance of English domination. As Boston's James Otis commented, "One single Act of Parliament . . . has set people thinking in six months, more than they had done in their whole lives."[19] One year later, the hated Stamp Act increased colonial anger against England. The Americans who had built thriving new communities now began to ask why they should suffer the harsh effects of decisions made by a Parliament that did not represent them and did not appear to have their best interests in mind.

3 Life in the Countryside

In the mid-eighteenth century, nine-tenths of the colonists—and virtually all of the Native Americans—lived in the countryside. This term included all areas outside of cities, towns, and villages, from long-settled farms to deep forests. The colonies' densely populated areas were situated along the seacoast and along navigable rivers. Beyond these places were farmland and the frontier. Familiar to Native Americans as traditional hunting grounds, the wild regions both frightened and attracted immigrants from crowded European countries. Colonial pioneers set out to tame the forests of this new land and to create fields and pastures for their crops and cattle.

The Ideal of the Farm

In spite of the endless labor involved in agriculture, letters and diaries from this period are filled with expressions of fondness for life on the farm. Recent arrivals from Europe were grateful for the opportunities that the wide-open spaces of the New World afforded them. Their lives as landowners—even if they faced the tremendous task of clearing virgin forest and planting crops—were far different from the experiences of the typical European peasant. In England, for example, only 20 percent of all farmworkers could ever hope to own their own farms. The other 80 percent lived out their lives as tenants or were itinerants, walking from place to place in search of work.

The founding fathers of the country, Thomas Jefferson and John Adams among them, looked on farming as the ideal way of life, the basis of the American economy. Jefferson thought that large-scale manufacturing would have a corrupting effect on the political and social fabric of the country. He favored instead an agricultural economy: "Those who labor in the earth are the chosen people of God."[20] Men like Jefferson and Adams bitterly regretted the time that they had to spend in the city as they built the new nation. Despite all of his other accomplishments, Jefferson wanted posterity to know him as a farmer.

Farming concerns were often uppermost in the minds of those who were away from home as elected representatives. In 1775 Josiah Bartlett, a delegate from New Hampshire to the Continental Congress, wrote to his wife:

> I am sorry to hear frost has Done Damage with you. I hope it has not Killed all the Beans &c. The Corn will Commonly Grow again. How is the flax in general like [likely] to be; what are like to be the Crops of hay with you; how is the winter and sumer grain like to be &c: Please write to me what is like to be the success of the farming business this year.[21]

Bartlett's desire for this information was more than simple curiosity. His family's welfare depended on the success of those crops.

The Farming Way of Life

Colonial farms ranged from small holdings to very large plantations. Yet there were many similarities in rural life, regardless of the size of the farm or the colony in which it was located.

Colonial farmers who could only grow enough food for their own households regarded themselves as fortunate compared to the landless peasants in the countries from which they or their ancestors had emigrated. Most colonial farmers, however, grew additional crops for sale. The fear of illness or injury motivated many farmers to earn and save some cash money by selling some of their produce.

For smaller farmers, informal exchanges—the barter system—often were more important than direct sales. Surplus hay might be given to a neighboring farmer in return for assistance in fencing a pasture. Even on the thinly settled frontier, farming households supported each other in ways unfamiliar to city dwellers.

In the eighteenth century city dwellers were becoming specialized in their work, pursuing only their own trade and buying whatever else they needed from other tradesmen, but most colonial farmers were still largely self-reliant. Because the population in rural areas was scattered and the economy undeveloped, most country folk built their own homes and farm buildings, made their own furniture, spun and wove their own cloth, and made their own clothes. They ate what they could produce on their own farm, and they relied on home cures for their illnesses.

Whether on the edge of the frontier or on established farmland, life was ruled by the necessity of completing agricultural tasks appropriate to each season of the year. Family members, servants (free or indentured), farmhands, and slaves worked during daylight hours to clear the land; care for livestock; plant, weed, and harvest crops; and to do all the other tasks involved in providing what they needed to eat and to wear. Storing crops, taking what could be sold to market,

The running of a small colonial farm required long hours of work from all members of the household. Sometimes, even neighbors were needed to pitch in.

weaving cloth, and cooking required time, effort, and skill, as did special tasks like butchering and making candles.

Types of Farms

While the average farm had about 100 acres, types of farms varied widely. In the southern colonies great plantations cultivated large tracts of land, usually through the use of slaves, to produce cash crops like tobacco, rice, sugar, and indigo for export. However, farms throughout the northern and the middle colonies were small, and even in the South many landholdings were no larger than could be cultivated by one farmer and his family. In the 1700s, 50 percent of the white population were subsistence farmers who had no slaves or indentured servants and worked the land themselves. Because of the scarcity of labor, farmers left fields fallow after the soil had been depleted by ten years of crops. Farmers would then wait twenty years for nutrients to be replenished naturally rather than trying to spread manure on a field to fertilize it.

A typical colonial farm grew corn, barley, and rye as well as many kinds of vegetables. Northerners grew white potatoes; Southerners grew sweet potatoes. Farm livestock included cattle and hogs for meat, for leather from the hides, and for milk and butter. Those who could afford horses used them to pull plows and farm wagons and to ride or to hitch to lighter wagons when the family wanted to travel. Sheep provided wool for spinning, weaving, and knitting, and most farms had some chickens as well. Many farms also included several acres of orchards, apple trees in the North and peaches and other fruit in the South.

To establish a farm, a settler needed a location that had both fresh water and trees. The trees could be cut to provide timber for a house and for fuel. The stumps and roots remaining in the ground made plowing impossible, especially since most new immigrants and small farmers lacked horses or oxen to perform this task. So instead, these farmers planted corn in little hillocks at six-foot intervals. The ground for this type of cultivation could be prepared by hand using a hoe, and twelve to fifteen hundred plants could be grown in each acre of land.

Since it was arduous to clear timber without the assistance of draft animals, small farmers often cultivated their land without cutting down the trees. Instead, they cut rings in the tree bark. This procedure, called "girdling," had been taught to the colonists by the Native Americans. Girdling kills the trees and allows sunlight to reach the ground under the leafless branches. Seeds could then be planted while the dead trees still stood, enabling the farmer to raise food without clearing the forest. Colonial farmers who were committed to permanent settlement and land ownership later cut down the dead trees as time and labor permitted, using the wood for fires and for fence building.

Zigzag fencing was constructed out of split rails, which could easily be moved as land use on the farm changed. Crops were fenced while cattle and hogs roamed free, foraging for themselves. Unfortunately, this left the livestock vulnerable to roaming wolves.

The Importance of Wood

The cutting down of forests didn't stop when a farmer had cleared his land. Wood, which was used as a building material and as fuel, was an important commodity in the colonies. In this new country, which saw its population double every twenty-five years, the need for houses, barns, and other kinds of buildings was constant. Essential buildings in the countryside included waterwheels and mills.

Subsistence farmers worked the land themselves and planted small crops for their own needs.

Causing the Grass to Grow

In his *Account of the History, Manners, and Customs of the Indian Nations, Who Once Inhabited Pennsylvania and the Neighbouring States*, John Heckewelder explained the Native American belief that the Great Spirit "made the earth and all that it contains for the common good of mankind; when he stocked the country that he gave them with plenty of game, it was not for the benefit of a few, but of all." This story, excerpted from *Travels in the American Colonies*, illustrates the clash of cultures that began when European colonists claimed ownership of land in the New World.

"Some travelling Indians having in the year 1777, put their horses over night to pasture in my little meadow, at Gnadenhutten on the Muskingum, I called on them in the morning to learn why they had done so. I endeavoured to make them sensible of the injury they had done me, especially as I intended to mow the meadow in a day or two.

Having finished my complaint, one of them replied: 'My friend, it seems you lay claim to the grass my horses have eaten, because you had enclosed it with a fence: now tell me, who caused the grass to grow? Can *you* make the grass grow? I think not, and no body can except the great Mannitto. He it is who causes it to grow both for my horses and yours! See, friend! the grass which grows out of the earth is common to all.

Say, did you never eat venison and bear's meat?—"Yes, very often."—Well, and did you ever hear me or any other Indian complain about that? No; then be not disturbed at my horses having eaten only once, of what you call *your* grass, though the grass my horses did eat, in like manner as the meat you did eat, was given to the Indians by the Great Spirit. Besides, if you will but consider, you will find that my horses did not eat *all* your grass. For friendship's sake, however, I shall never put my horses in your meadow again.'"

Often built completely of wood, mills captured the power of water falling down riverbeds and sent it through wooden gears and crankshafts to run saws for cutting more timber and planks. Building with wood was much faster than using brick or stone. Canals, bridges (including the wooden truss bridge), and some roads were constructed of wood as the interior areas were opened to settlement. Coopers used wood for making the casks and barrels in which all products were sold, and timber itself was a significant export from the colonies.

Colonial farmers were experts in working with wood, clearing their land, building their own houses, and cutting the shingles for their roofs. Many colonial farmers spent winters creating shingles to sell to city dwellers or to send to European markets. Farm families, and most other colonists as well, used wood for cooking and heating. Wood fires also smelted iron. Not a farm product, wood was nevertheless a resource relied on by farmers and everyone else in the colonies.

Women on the Farm

The small-farm family was led by a man who, assisted by his sons, would do the work that required the greatest physical labor. But every woman on a colonial farm also had vital tasks to perform. Frequently mothers and daughters worked in the fields, especially at harvest time, when everyone rushed to gather the ripened crops. Women usually were responsible for gardening, raising vegetables, and preserving food to eat during the winter. At slaughtering time, women prepared and preserved the meat. Caring for chickens and milking cows were also regarded as women's work, as was the heavy labor of drawing water out of the well and carrying it into the house.

As housekeepers, women cooked, knitted, and sewed a significant proportion of the clothing for the household, cleaned the clothes, and performed many other duties

Drawing water from the well and carrying it back to the house was only one of countless tasks performed by colonial women.

around the home. It was also the responsibility of women to raise the children, often serving as their teachers and physicians as well as their mothers. These tasks continued day in and day out, an unending round of work that kept most women close to hearth and home.

Some women who lived on larger farms and plantations also became responsible for financial and management duties, especially if their husbands were ill or away from home. Abigail Adams, for example, had to manage the operations of the Adams farm as the years of her husband's public service in the Continental Congress stretched on. Many such women learned to budget funds for wages, plan the entire cycle of planting and harvesting, and hire responsible laborers to carry out these tasks. Even the wives of poor farmers sometimes engaged in business dealings as they sold butter, eggs, and other produce.

Life on a Plantation

Although geographically isolated on their large holdings, plantation families tended to identify with one another and to cooperate in raising and marketing their crops. The planter would generally plan the farming year—what crops were to be grown, where they were to be planted, how they were to be sold—while the slaves carried out the work. On most plantations, the white owners were far outnumbered by their black slaves. This was a very different life from the experience of the small farming family.

Thomas Jefferson, the lover of liberty, was born into the Virginia culture of slave ownership and tobacco plantations. He owned 187 slaves, and on his isolated plantation, Monticello, he created an almost self-sufficient community. Jefferson's slaves carried

As the men of the colonies met in Philadelphia in the months leading up to the Declaration of Independence, their wives and families bore the responsibility for managing life at home. In May 1776 Abigail Adams wrote a letter (reprinted in L. H. Butterfield's *The Book of Abigail and John*) to her husband, John, to tell him how she was managing in his absence. She paid her workers in "pounds," the British unit of currency used throughout the colonies.

"We have had fine Spring rains which makes the Husbandry [business of farming] promise fair—but the great difficulty has been to procure Laborours. There is such a demand of Men from the public and such a price given that the farmer who Hires must be greatly out of pocket. A man will not talk to you who is worth hireing under 24 pounds per year. . . . Isaac insisted upon my giving him 20 pounds or he would leave me. He is no mower and I found very unfit to take the lead upon the Farm, having no forethought or any contrivance to plan his Business, tho in the Execution faithfull.

I found I want somebody of Spirit who was wiser than myself, to conduct my Business. I went about my Friends and inquired but every Labourer who was active was gone and going into the Service [militia]. . . . Mr. Belcher is now with me and has undertaken to conduct the Business, which he has hitherto done with Spirit and activity. I know his virtues and I know his faults. . . .

I am still in quest of a Man by the year, but whether I shall effect it, I know not. I have done the best I could. We are just now ready to plant, the barly look[s] charmingly, I shall be quite a Farmeress [woman farmer] another year."

Abigail Adams, the wife of John Adams, managed the family farm while her husband served in the Continental Congress.

Monticello, Thomas Jefferson's Virginian home, was a large plantation in the South.

out farming and gardening tasks to feed the people and animals. They also made nails, built barrels for storage, and worked as carpenters and masons to construct the many buildings on the property. They fenced the pastures, cleared the woods, and hauled heavy loads of produce to market or to be shipped abroad. Other important tasks included making shoes, spinning wool, weaving cloth and blankets, cleaning, and cooking.

Unfortunately, many slaveholders were neither as benevolent nor as enlightened as Thomas Jefferson. They owned slaves to perform heavy labor, and they enforced this requirement harshly. Some owners gave their slaves individual tasks and allowed them to have free time once the daily assignment was completed. After working dawn to dusk for their masters, slaves were also typically required to grow their own food. Many slaves were organized into work gangs watched over by hated overseers who could administer cruel punishments like whipping. Labor began at dawn and continued until dusk, stopping only for a meal of fried cornmeal in the middle of the day. The harshness and misery of this life far exceeded the experiences of even the poorest free person in the New World.

Taming the Wilderness

By 1770 well-established farm communities existed from Maine to Georgia, but only within one hundred miles of the seacoast. Beyond that region, colonial farmers were considered pioneers. They faced hostility from Native Americans, whose hunting grounds they were unknowingly destroying, and they needed to be even more self-sufficient than other colonists. Great perils faced those traveling through the "trackless wilderness" to the new homestead or returning for a short visit once the growing season was done.

Life in the Countryside

Roads and bridges had yet to be built anywhere except in the most settled regions. Pioneering families often had to cut a way through the forest as they went, which proved to be a slow and exhausting mode of travel. Injuries to travelers and damage to wagons were frequent occurrences. Even more difficult was the danger of getting lost in the vast areas with little sign of habitation by Europeans. Few maps existed, and they were available only to the wealthy. In this period, travelers could also be threatened by the attacks of wild animals. In South Carolina an act was passed that offered a reward to "whatsoever white person by himself or slave shall destroy and kill wolfs, tyger [panther], beare or wild catt."[22] It would be many years before what Americans think of as "the frontier" moved over the Appalachian Mountains and into the West.

A Lonely Life

Pioneers who penetrated into wilderness areas experienced great loneliness and missed the sense of community that developed between farmers in more settled areas. One young pioneer, John Reynolds, left his family and relatives while he and his father worked for a summer carving a new farm out of the wilderness. When his father left the farm to fetch the rest of the family, John, who was fifteen, had to stay alone for several months.

In the Upper Part of Virginia

In 1753 a small group of Moravians left Bethlehem, Pennsylvania, and traveled to Wachovia, North Carolina. The Moravians were a Bohemian sect seeking land where they could live in safety. One member of this group wrote a diary, reprinted in Newton D. Mereness's *Travels in the American Colonies*, describing the Moravians' adventures on their six-week journey. They had no clear directions or map to guide their steps, and they often had great difficulty finding food and shelter for themselves and fodder and water for their horses. Frequently they discovered that they had taken a difficult path when an easier one was nearby. They relied on help from friendly planters along the way.

"It was warm and sultry weather and we found no water in the eleven miles between our last night camp, and this place. It is 200 miles to Williamsburg, the capital of Virginia.

We went a mile and a half further to a tavern keeper named Severe and inquired about our way, but could get no definite information. Three and a half miles beyond, the road forked. The Brethren Gottlob and Nathanael took the left-hand road and found a woman who told them about it; they returned and we took the right-hand road, but found no water for ten miles.

It grew late, and we had to drive ten miles into the night to find a stopping place. We had to climb two miles where everyone had to help push or we could not have made it, for our horses were quite exhausted. Two Brethren had to keep a little ahead to seek out the road; and so we came at last to Thomas Harris' plantation, where we bought food for our horses, and set up our tent a little way from the house. The people were friendly and assisted the travelers gladly."

I had not a book, not a scrap of printed paper. I had one letter from my uncle Edward to my father . . . that I oft-times read. Each day I cut a notch in the door cheek, and on Sabbath one of double size. Thus I kept tally of the days and weeks, and often counted the notches to pass the time, which hung so heavy. Every night the wolves howled around my cabin, and the owls hooted—discordant noises, well fitted to nurture melancholy.[23]

Even the family cow was lonely. After her long trek to reach the little Reynolds cabin, the cow was unwilling to stay there and ran away several times to the nearest neighboring barn. John wrote, "Having no company she would not stay with us. We could not drive nor lead her home. After we had got her part of the way she broke from us and ran back."[24] The family finally had to sell their lonely cow to the neighbor.

Militias

The wilderness of the New World had always seemed like a lonely and dangerous place to European settlers. In response to the isolation and danger, the early English colonists in Virginia, Plymouth, Massachusetts Bay, and Connecticut set up volunteer militias that were influenced by English military tradition. Drawing on the experience of English colonists in Ireland, the American colonists lived within wooden fortifications and depended on their militias for protection. As time advanced, most colonies expanded their militias, encouraging young men to play their part in protecting their neighbors' property. Only Pennsylvania, influenced by the pacifist beliefs of the Quakers, had no law establishing a militia until 1777.

For rural colonists, the militia was of more than military significance. Each month the militia would meet to carry out their exercises; these monthly meetings became social events, bringing the isolated farming families together. As they watched the men run through their drill, the women talked and the children enjoyed the opportunity of playing with other youngsters. A generation later, this militia tradition would enable the colonies to fight a successful war of rebellion against Great Britain, which at that time was the most powerful nation on the earth.

As farmers tamed the wilderness, they created a new way of life. The great fertility of so much land in America helped build the nation in ways that few individual farmers could have foreseen. Far from the ferment and political discussions taking place in colonial cities, the independent people of the countryside were nevertheless contributing to the forces leading to the coming break from domination by Great Britain.

Home and Hearth

In colonial times almost everyone lived in a family, or, more precisely, in a family group that included the persons related by blood along with servants, farmhands, and sometimes slaves. The people who inhabited the thirteen colonies relied on each other. From birth to death, a colonial person was provided for by the family and in turn worked for the welfare of the others in the household. Food, clothing, and shelter were no more important than the sense of belonging the family gained by the way in which they lived and worked.

European colonists retained a family image that had more in common with feudal ways of life than with modern notions of family. Instead of thinking of extended blood relations as family, American colonials reserved the term for the people that lived on the same land, worked together, and only secondarily were of the same lineage.

Despite close, loving relationships that show clearly in colonial letters and diaries, the emotions that cement modern families together were less important to a colonial person than the fact that the household—on subsistence farms or great plantations—worked and lived together on the same land. William Byrd II, one of the largest plantation owners in Virginia, wrote a letter to the earl of Orrery in which he explained what his life was like:

> I have a large family of my own. Like one of the patriarchs, I have my flocks and my herds, my bond-men and bond-women [slaves]. . . . I must take care to keep all my people to their duty, to set all the springs in motion, and to make everyone draw his equal share to carry the machine forward.[25]

Byrd considered his "bond-men and bond-women" to be part of his family. He saw himself not as a loving father but as a person responsible for setting work in motion and for keeping the other persons in the household to their tasks.

In New England the "family" was also a unit that worked together. In Puritan times the men in charge of a town would assign a single man to join a family if he were living alone. The Puritans believed they were following a biblical rule set down in Psalm 68: "God setteth the solitary in families." New England architecture also reflected this larger sense of family. Colonial houses typically had ells, lean-tos, and other additions to provide room for a growing household of married children and hired hands. Although apprentices and indentured servants were included under the term *family*, relatives not living in the household were excluded. Instead, they were "kith [neighbors] and kin"— important people, but not as close as those living and working under one roof.

Marriage Customs

In the Old World, a marriage was likely to be arranged as much for the overall welfare of

A colonial household not only consisted of blood relations, but servants and farmhands as well. All worked together to maintain the livelihood of the owners.

the family as it was to suit the desires of the bride and groom. This practice was changing in the colonies as the eighteenth century progressed. John Adams wrote a letter to one of his daughters as she seemed to be choosing an inappropriate husband (in her father's eyes, anyway). Adams's letter shows that he had assumed he would be able, as a father, to select her mate: "Take care how you dispose your heart—I hoped to be at home and to have chosen a partner for you. Or at least to have given you some good Advise before you should choose."[26]

Having run away from Boston as a seventeen-year-old, Benjamin Franklin did not have the benefit of parental advice as he considered his own marriage. This passage from his *Autobiography* shows that Franklin saw marriage as more than simply a love-based relationship, although he also liked the girl he was considering marrying. Her relatives seem to have had an equally commercial perspective on the proposal:

Mrs. Godfrey projected a Match for me with a Relation's Daughter, took Opportuni-

ties of bringing us often together, till a serious Courtship on my Part ensu'd, the Girl being in herself very deserving. The old Folks encourag'd me by continual Invitations to Supper, and by leaving us together, Till at length it was time to explain. Mrs. Godfrey manag'd our little Treaty. I let her know that I expected as much Money with their Daughter as would pay off my Remaining Debt for the Printing-house, which I believe was not then above a Hundred Pounds. She brought me Word they had no such Sum to spare. I said they might mortgage their House in the Loan Office. The Answer to this after some Days was that they did not approve the Match; that on Enquiry . . . they had been inform'd the Printing Business was not a profitable one . . . and therefore I was forbidden the House and the Daughter shut up.[27]

Finding a Marriage Partner

Like Benjamin Franklin, many colonial men had difficulty finding someone to marry. In

Although the early colonies discouraged the practice of arranged marriages, the future bride and groom still needed to request permission to marry from their fathers. Here a colonial couple walks to church together.

the early years of a settlement, there were usually many more men than women. Single women who migrated to the colonies as indentured servants often found their fates easier than those of single men. Marriage to a master released many female immigrants from their indenture bonds.

For slaves, marriage was even more difficult. Far more African males than females lived in bondage in the American colonies, and, of course, slaves were not free to travel in search of a mate. Furthermore, finding a marriage partner was more challenging for northern slaves than for southern ones, in spite of the fact that their lives were gener-

ally easier. Northern slaves typically lived in the same house as their owners and were adequately fed and clothed. However, northern families rarely owned more than one or two slaves. These slaves had very few opportunities to meet potential marriage partners. In addition, slaves newly arrived in the colonies did not always find it easy to form bonds with other blacks, who were likely to be from different African homelands or language groups.

Despite these handicaps, slaves made great efforts to marry and create families. Some of these marriages were supported by the slave owners while others were disregarded, especially when one member of the family was sold to another owner. Thomas Jefferson, a relatively kindly master, encouraged his female slaves to establish happy relationships. He gave the women "a pot and a bed, which I always promise them when they take husbands at home."[28] These were in addition to the beds, blankets, pots, sifters for flour and meal, hats, stockings, and shoes that Jefferson's slaves received from time to time. They were also given cloth and clothing twice a year.

Childhood in the Colonies

Eighteenth-century marriage customs were very different from modern ones, but they usually led to happy, committed marriages. In the same way, colonial parents had certain harsh beliefs concerning child rearing, but they still rejoiced in their children. From New York, Edward Chandler wrote to his brother-in-law Sam about his baby daughter: "Oh, Samy, she is the loveliest Child that ever god created. There is nothing in the world half so dear to me as my child."[29]

Yet colonial families feared spoiling their children and took care to bring them up to be respectful, hardworking adults. Children from European American families were dressed as little adults and began working with their parents as soon as they were able. Even relatively wealthy families expected their children to keep busy with studies and chores. Wealthy Anna Green Winslow of Boston could bake pies at age eleven and was entrusted with this responsibility for Thanksgiving dinner. She also could make "fine network," knit lace, spin linen thread and woolen yarn, make pocketbooks, weave watch strings, sew, and piece patchwork for quilts. Under the watchful eye of her Aunt Deming, she strove to do all these things "true," or neatly and well. In 1772 she wrote to her mother:

I have spun 30 knots of linen yarn and (partly) new footed a pair of stockings for Lucinda, read a part of the pilgrim's progress, coppied part of my text journal . . . play'd some, tuck'd [sewed decorative tucks in cloth] a great deal (Aunt Deming says it is very true) laugh'd enough, & I tell aunt it is all human nature, if not human reason. And now, I wish my honored mamma a very good night.[30]

Clearly all this housework and studying did not break Anna's buoyant spirit. She was eager for her aunt's approval, and she formally honored her mother, but she made jokes for them, too, and wrote to her parents in faraway Nova Scotia that she "laughed enough."

Learning Proper Behavior

Many colonial parents believed it was their duty to bring their children up to be respectable, thoughtful, and God-fearing. They enforced strict rules of behavior and expected their children to show them respect at all times. Anna Green Winslow's addressing her mother as "honored mamma" is an example of her obedience to this expectation. Colonial boys also received a great deal of instruction on behavior and proper attitudes. The lessons even covered what to do—and what not to do—on the walk home from school:

Run not Hastily in the Street, nor go too Slowly. Wag not to and fro, nor use any Antic Postures either of the Head, Hands, Feet or Body. Through [throw] not aught [anything] on the Street, as Dirt or Stones. If thou meetest the scholars of any other School, jeer not nor affront them, but show them love and respect and quietly pass along.[31]

Colonial children were taught adult tasks as soon as they were old enough and were expected to behave properly. Girls acquired countless skills at an early age so they could carry out their household duties efficiently in adulthood.

At the beginning of the colonial period, the efforts of families to control and restrain their children began at birth. As Europeans did, they swaddled their infants tightly, wrapping them in cloths attached to a board so that their bodies would grow straight and they would never crawl on all fours "like a wild beast." During the eighteenth century, European Americans abandoned the practice and allowed their babies to move and crawl actively.

Colonial Clothing

Adults in colonial times wore clothing that only gradually evolved from European styles. Some of the garments worn in colonial times have disappeared from use; others appear in altered form in styles worn two hundred years later. As with their houses, colonial people had different types and qualities of clothing depending on their social class and their wealth. The rich could import silken garments from Europe, but most others depended on what could be produced in the colonies, either by their own family members or for sale if they lived near a city.

Women's Attire

For work or when she wanted to be informal, the middle-class colonial woman wore a shift (similar to a modern slip but long and full), a corset that had shoulder straps, a petticoat, and an apron. Some women went barefoot while others wore thin white stockings. They wore white linen caps on their heads, always covered by a straw hat out of doors. To be more formal, the colonial woman added to these garments a jacket, which grew longer as fashions changed. Upper-class women wore elaborate silk brocade gowns for formal occasions. Gloves and a fan were part of this outfit, as was a lace-trimmed cap. Sarah Kemble Knight of Boston described in her journal the manner in which New York women dressed in 1704:

> The English goe very fashionable in their dress. But the Dutch, especially the middling sort, differ from our women in their habit so loose, wear French muches, which are like a Cap and a head band in one, leaving their Ears bare, which are sett out with Jewells of a large size and

Fashion on Sudbury Street

Without TV and magazines, eighteenth-century country people had little idea of what fashions were like in the cities. In a letter to her mother in Nova Scotia, Anna Green Winslow describes the embarrassment of being dressed unfashionably in Boston in 1771. This excerpt is taken from the *Diary of Anna Green Winslow*.

"I hope aunt wont let me wear the black hatt with the red Dominie—for the people will ask me what I have got to sell as I go along street if I do, or, how do the folk at New guinie do? Dear mamma, you don't know the fashion here—I beg to look like other folk. You don't know what a stir it would be made in sudbury street, were I to make my appearance there in my red Dominie & black Hatt. But the old cloak & bonnett together will make me a decent bonnett for common ocation . . . it's a pitty some of the ribbins you sent wont do for the Bonnet."

Attending a formal ball at the Westover House, wealthy men and women dress in their best attire.

many in number. And their fingers hoop'd with Rings, some with large stones in them of many Coullers [colors] as were their pendants in their ears, which You should see very old women wear as well as young.[32]

What Men Wore

Like women's fashions, men's clothing varied depending on the wealth and social class of the wearer. Slaves, especially in hot areas, often had only a shapeless garment of linsey-woolsey, a rough fabric woven out of linen and wool. Many slaves went barefoot. Poor whites had a little more to wear, as is shown by the clothing sent to the first colonists living in settlements in Georgia. In addition to a heavy outer coat, the men received "a Frock [lightweight coat] and Trowsers of Lintsey Wolsey, A Shirt, Frock and Trowsers of Osnabrig [coarse cloth], A Pair of Shoes from England and Two Pairs of Country Shoes."[33]

The trousers sent to the Georgia colonists were for farmworkers; upper-class men wore knee breeches and stockings. Their clothing included a three-piece suit, which changed gradually in length and outline during the eighteenth century. Nevertheless, the coat, vest, and pants ensemble has endured; a modern version is worn today by businessmen in most countries of the world (minus the vest in warmer climates). The colonial garments came in far more colors than today's suits, and at some periods the vests reached the knees. Colonial men's jackets often had sweeping skirts and deep cuffs with large buttons.

Another eighteenth-century men's fashion—the powdered wig—is still worn today by judges and lawyers in legal systems with a British heritage. Heavy and awkward, the wig established that the wearer had a high social position and did not have to do manual labor. Whether long or short, the wig was uncomfortable to wear and expensive to maintain. Men and boys had to take lessons in holding their heads up properly under the mass of canvas and powdered horsehair; if they moved too fast, the wig could fall off and reveal the shaved head underneath. With the coming of the American Revolution, men abandoned wigs, grew out their hair, and wore it in ponytails.

Obtaining Food in Colonial America

Bending over her open hearth and working with the simplest of pots and pans, the colonial housewife produced meals from food grown or slaughtered on the farm, bought at a market, hunted in the woods, or fished from the sea. Immigrants had to learn how to find food in their new environment and to prepare the unfamiliar Indian corn in place of the familiar European strains of wheat, which did not grow well in the New World.

Some pioneer families lived nine months of the year on venison, and the hunters also brought back hares, squirrels, turkeys, pigeons, ducks, and geese. The Pilgrims were amazed by the variety of seafood to be caught in and around Massachusetts Bay, which boasted two hundred kinds of fish and shellfish. Coastal families salted fish to preserve it for the winter, and they caught lobsters weighing five or six pounds and oysters up to thirteen inches long. In addition, the Wampanoag Indians showed the early settlers how to dig clams, another valuable food source.

Cooking Methods

As was true with clothing, colonial families ate different diets depending on their wealth. On subsistence farms, everyone in the household, including a slave or hired hand, ate the same meal, which was cooked in one pot and combined hominy, other vegetables, and meat. (Hominy consists of hulled, dried corn kernels, which require long boiling to become tender enough to eat.) Other slaves were fed hopping John, made of grits (coarsely ground corn) and peas.

A colonial woman prepares a stew in a large pot over a fire. Colonial families' meals differed throughout the colonies but corn was an important dietary staple.

Corn, in its many forms, was an important food, as were pumpkin and squash. Immigrants learned from the Native Americans how to make certain foods that are still popular today, including roasted ears of fresh corn and popcorn. Cornbread was made with dried huckleberries, and colonial cooks also prepared succotash, a mixture of corn and beans. Words like *hominy* and *succotash* are reminders of the Indian origin of these dishes. The Europeans did not like to eat the Indian foods made with pumpkin, but squash (another Indian word) was used in many ways.

Special Dishes

The familiar apple appeared in pies and many other dishes. In addition, colonial housewives picked herbs, fruits, and nuts in the countryside. They preserved much of this harvest and their garden vegetables by pickling samphire (a wild herb), purple cabbage, nasturtium buds, green walnuts, lemons, radish pods, barberries, elder buds, parsley, mushrooms, asparagus, and many kinds of fish and fruit. Meat was salted and pickled in a large container; if the family had a smokehouse, they could smoke beef and pork to preserve them. Making sausages and headcheese also allowed colonial families—who had no refrigeration—to preserve meat for the winter.

In spite of this apparent abundance, European Americans longed for luxury foods like sugar, coffee, tea, and spices. These imported items were extremely expensive and often taxed by the British government. Some kinds of food may have been abundant during certain times of the year, but feeding a household was never an easy task. In the city the monetary cost of food was usually high, and in the countryside the family devoted most of their time and effort to obtaining and preparing food. Some colonial families were grateful for the bubbling pot of stew that hung on an iron hook over their open hearth; others offered thanks for their meal to a gracious host and hostess who set out a sideboard covered with many elaborately prepared dishes in the elegant dining room of their mansion.

The close, hardworking families of colonial times represent an ideal that has had a permanent influence on the society that they created. As immigrants built the cities, towns, and farms of the New World, they also developed new social customs, a strong respect for hard work, and an independent way of life for the growing nation. In some ways the changes brought by modern times have been less important to American society than the heritage established by those who lived and worked in this country during the colonial period.

Crafts, Skills, and Professions

Colonial Americans placed a high value on work. While the great majority of people in the colonies lived in the countryside as farmers or hunters, the towns and cities had a growing population of artisans, craftsmen, and laborers. These people used their specialized skills to produce goods for sale. At the beginning of the eighteenth century, each piece was crafted separately by hand, but technological improvements and mass production techniques were transforming the manufacturing process. Larger colonial industries included mining, construction, and maritime commerce. These industries employed many people with specialized skills. Nonfarmworkers also included people who practiced the learned professions: ministers, doctors, and lawyers. Along with wealth, these workers helped create the self-reliant attitudes that led the colonies toward independence.

The Artisan's Workshop

As on the farm, the family was the basic unit of production in a colonial workshop. Production tasks were typically carried out in a building that also served as the family's home. The business owner's children grew up with the family's trade, learning by observing and helping out with whatever tasks they could perform. Many colonial wives were so involved in these businesses that they could carry on with the work after they were widowed.

In certain ways work in colonial times was heavy, tiring, and labor-intensive. However, masters of this period expected their workers to complete set tasks rather than to labor continuously for an eight-hour shift. The colonial workshop and family home provided a sheltering sense of acceptance and community, usually employing one or two, but rarely more than ten, workers in addition to the blood relatives. All were treated as family members, receiving care during illnesses and training in the needed skills.

The Master's Responsibilities

The master of a colonial workshop had many responsibilities, both for the conduct of the business and for the welfare of the household that worked in it. It was the master's job to see that the shop was built, equipped with tools, and supplied with materials. He also designed the product, taught his workers how to make it, and supervised its production. In addition, the master had to find customers. Items requiring expensive materials and a high level of skill to produce were typically expensive. Each would be created to order for a specific buyer who had commissioned the production of a cherrywood secretary; a silver porringer, or bowl; a grandfather clock; or even a pair of shoes.

Workshops operated similarly to trade schools. There were two classes of workers in different stages of the learning process. Ap-

Men work in a colonial shop in Jamestown, Virginia. Workers had certain tasks assigned to them and received training from the master of the shop.

prentices usually joined the workshop as young teenagers. They worked under contracts that were similar to indentures and bound the boys to serve the master for a specific term, usually seven years. In return, the master was responsible for the apprentices' education, housing, room, board, and clothing. When these boys successfully passed through their apprenticeship, they became journeymen. The journeymen also lived in the household until they were ready to become masters themselves, but they earned a small wage, unlike the apprentices.

Working Together

Throughout the workday, everyone in the workshop would stop for occasional light meals, usually accompanied by beer or cider. When customers came to buy goods, they would be invited to share in the refreshments. Singing and talking made the workshop's labor go faster. Sometimes one apprentice would be assigned to read the newspaper out loud as the rest of the workers completed their tasks. In cities, the craft workshops were often located near each other. Masters would assist others in the same craft, jobbing out extra work and sharing workers and materials from time to time. Given the difficulties of transportation in the colonies, this last form of exchange was important to almost all artisans.

Colonial Industries

During the mid–eighteenth century, other significant changes in colonial work patterns resulted from the growth of large industries—mining, construction, and maritime commerce. These major enterprises were factors in the move toward wage labor and away from the master-apprentice system. Colonial industrialists found ways to increase productivity and profits as more and more business operations began taking place outside of the family workplace.

By the 1770s the colonies had more than 250 ironworks concentrated in southwestern New York, northern New Jersey, eastern Pennsylvania, and northern Maryland. They were already producing one-seventh of the world's iron. A colonial ironworks established

Ben Franklin's Apprenticeship

When Benjamin Franklin's brother John reached adulthood, he left the family's tallow chandlery (candle-making business) and set up his own business in Rhode Island. His father wanted twelve-year-old Ben to take John's place. In his *Autobiography*, reprinted in George McMichael's *Anthology of American Literature*, Franklin described what happened.

"But my Dislike to the Trade continuing, my Father was under Apprehensions that if he did not find one for me more agreable, I should break away and get to Sea, as his son Josiah had done to his great Vexation. He therefore sometimes took me to walk with him, and see Joiners [woodworkers], Bricklayers, Turners [lathe workers], Braziers [brass workers], &c. at their Work, that he might observe my Inclination, and endeavour to fix it on some Trade or other on Land. It has ever since been useful to me, having learnt so much by it, as to be able to do little Jobs my self in my House, when a workman could not readily be got; and to construct little Machines for my Experiments while the Intention of making the Experiment was fresh and warm in my mind. . . .

From a child I was fond of Reading, and all the little Money that came into my Hands was ever laid out in Books. . . . This Bookish Inclination at length determin'd my Father to make me a Printer, tho' he already had one son, James, of that profession. In 1717 my Brother James return'd from England with a Press and Letters to set up his Business in Boston. . . . My Father was impatient to have me apprenticed to my Brother. I stood out for some time, but at last was persuaded and signed the Indentures, when I was yet but 12 years old. I was to serve as an Apprentice till I was 21 Years of Age, only I was to be allow'd Journeyman's Wages during the last Year."

Benjamin Franklin served his apprenticeship in his brother's printing shop.

near a source of iron ore resembled a small town. Wood from the surrounding forest was cut and made into the charcoal needed to fuel the furnaces, and the produce of a company-owned farm fed the workers. Carpenters built housing and wagons, working with blacksmiths, wheelwrights, and cartwrights. The ironworks became an almost self-sufficient community with stores, gristmills, sawmills, and shops.

The Building Trades

Building the new industries and communities in the American colonies required many thousands of construction workers. These included carpenters, joiners, masons, glaziers, housewrights, millwrights, roofers, and laborers. The master carpenter was responsible for the successful completion of the project, often serving as the building's designer as well. The joiner built the parts: windows, doors, and staircases. The hand plane and the adze helped him create the intricate shapes out of a piece of timber. Some of these workers were itinerant, walking from place to place in search of buildings to erect for farmers and townspeople. Other construction workers spent their entire lives in one of the colonial cities, building to meet the needs of the rapidly expanding population.

The Learned Professions

The world of work in the American colonies also included the professions. Growing communities needed ministers, lawyers, and physicians. Despite the demand, obtaining schooling in these professions was difficult in the New World because few universities existed. Training was far more often a matter of apprenticeship than of a formal course of education.

Large industries grew in the colonies during the mid–eighteenth century. Such industries included colonial ironworks, which became one of the largest of the new enterprises.

Given their commitment to their religious beliefs, the colonists were anxious to provide ministers for their churches. However, transatlantic travel was so dangerous that fathers were reluctant to send their sons abroad to study. Instead, colonists established colleges of their own. By the time of the American Revolution, seven colleges were established in the colonies. All soon broadened their missions to educate students belonging to different sects and did not limit their courses to theological studies.

Harvard in Massachusetts, Yale in Connecticut, and William and Mary in Virginia were all founded to serve the established churches of their colonies, respectively producing Puritan, Congregationalist, and Anglican clergymen. Princeton was built by New-Side Presbyterians and Brown by Revivalist Baptists. Rutgers was the college of the Dutch Reformed Church, while Dartmouth had begun as an Indian mission and later became Congregationalist. The Anglicans and

Crafts, Skills, and Professions

Harvard College in Massachusetts was founded to produce Puritan clergymen. Pictured here in 1770, Harvard remains one of the most prestigious universities today.

Presbyterians worked together to found King's College in New York, later Columbia, as well as the College of Pennsylvania, which later became the University of Pennsylvania. This college had the first chair of botany and natural history in the colonies, and it gave the first systematic instruction in medicine. These colleges trained ministers for the colonies' churches, but they also enabled young men to get other types of education.

The Practice of Law

Separated from the Old World traditions that demanded long university educations and formal legal apprenticeships for attorneys, colonial people had to create a legal system and its practitioners as best they could. In England lawyers were trained to handle specific types of cases. In America, however, lawyers were educated to handle any legal matter that arose. Men who hoped to practice law gained the required knowledge and expertise by apprenticing themselves to practicing lawyers and gaining as wide an experience as possible.

Many of the colonies' leading politicians were lawyers who were accustomed to discussing ideas and solving many kinds of prob-

lems as they carried out their profession. For example, once Thomas Jefferson finished his apprenticeship and was admitted to the Virginia bar, he worked on land contracts, cases concerning cattle eating others' crops, disputed wills, the administration of estates, and sometimes even assault and battery.

John Adams wrote about the demands of his legal education in his autobiography. In 1758 he asked Mr. Gridley, the most important man practicing law in Boston, how he could get the education he needed. First, Gridley asked Adams about his general education and his writing skills.

> Then Mr. Gridley run [made] a comparison between the business and studies of a lawyer, a gentleman of the bar in England and those of one here: a lawyer in this country must study common law, and civil law, and natural law, and admiralty law; and must do the duty of a counsellor, a lawyer, an attorney, a solicitor, and even of a scrivener; so that the difficulties of the profession are much greater here than in England.[34]

Adams wrote that in learning to be a lawyer he "suffered very much from want of books." Yet the practice of law was less technical than in England, for few colonial judges were well educated. As one lawyer said of the chief justice of New Hampshire, "Judge Livermore, having no learning himself, did not like to be pestered with it in his courts." When the lawyer tried to read an argument to the judge from a law book, Livermore only asked if the lawyer "thought that he and his brethren [the other judges] did not know as much as those musty old worm-eaten books." [35]

On the other hand, many nonlawyers were aware of legal principles; they understood and claimed their legal rights. This attitude was a factor in the colonies' increasing unhappiness with unfair acts of Parliament. One observer at the time said, "Generally in our colonies, particularly in New-England, people are much addicted to quirks in the law; a very ordinary country man in New-England is almost qualified for a country-attorney in England." [36]

Physicians

The practice of medicine in the colonies also had a homespun quality. There were only a few physicians with training in European medicine. At this time, European doctors tended to search for one simple idea that would explain all the workings of the human body and account for all the diseases. In Europe this theorizing was not usually accompanied by practical research into what was actually effective in treating illness.

Furthermore, many of the medications prepared according to European physicians' elaborate recipes were harmful or actually poisonous. Some contained lead, urine, or other dangerous substances. In addition, medical training was reserved for upper-class men who could afford an expensive university education, and frequently the graduates did not wish to involve themselves directly with patient care. These physicians preferred to develop abstract theories and were reluctant to come in close contact with lower-class people, whether or not they were suffering from an illness. Some of their prescriptions, administered by others, were called "heroic" because they were so harsh. European doctors commonly recommended bleeding the sufferers or purging their digestive systems to remove harmful "humors" (the imaginary fluids blamed for causing illness).

New World medicine had none of these aristocratic or intellectual trappings. Much

Thomas Jefferson Becomes a Lawyer

Thomas Jefferson studied law briefly during his two years at college, but his real professional training took place in the law office of George Wythe, who practiced law as well as taught at William and Mary. Jefferson said that Wythe was "my second father, my antient master, my earliest & best friend." As quoted in Wendell D. Garrett's *The Worlds of Thomas Jefferson*, Jefferson left the following advice for other law students.

"In reading the reporters, enter in a commonplace book every case of value, condensed into the narrowest possible compass which will admit of presenting distinctly the principle of the case. This operation is doubly useful, insomuch as it obliges the student to seek out the pith of the case, and habituates him to a condensation of thought and to an acquisition of the most valuable of all the talents, that of never using two words when one will do."

A colonial doctor sits by his patient's bed. Colonial doctors used practical and generally unharmful treatments on their patients.

medical care was prescribed by ministers, who avoided heroic measures; rather, colonial physician-ministers often called for bed rest, fresh air, and massages. Whether or not these methods cured the patients, at least they did no harm.

Treating Smallpox

The minister of the Old South Church, Thomas Thacher, wrote a simple manual to guide those caring for people with smallpox, a deadly disease that ravaged colonial and Native American communities. It was reprinted several times in the eighteenth century. Thacher made it clear that he was not a physician but was a "well wisher to the sick." Yet modern physicians agree that, for the time, his prescriptions were sensible:

> As soon as this disease therefore appears by its signs, let the sick abstein from Flesh [meat] and wine, and open Air, let him use [drink] small beare [beer] for his ordinary drink, and moderately when he desires it. For food use water-gruel, water-potage, and other things having no manifest hot quality, easy of digestion, boild Apples, and milk sometimes for change, but the coldness taken off.[37]

Often medical care was provided by someone with no medical training at all. Both George Washington and Thomas Jefferson provided the medical care for their slaves and other household members. Jefferson personally inoculated seventy of the people on his plantation against smallpox. These planters applied their common sense and self-reliance to the problem of protecting their households.

The challenges of making a living in the 1750s produced a nation of skilled, self-reliant people. As the communities of the New World became more established, those who lived in them worked together to build their skills and support each other in developing a uniquely American way of life.

CHAPTER 6

Science, Technology, and Health

Throughout the Western world, the eighteenth century was an age of scientific investigation and technological advancement. Science was separating itself from philosophical speculation, alchemy (an early chemical theory that centered around the idea that nonprecious metals could be transformed into gold), and superstition. In addition, the world of work was changing as a result of discoveries about the physical properties of materials and the development of efficient production methods. The American colonies participated in this movement, spurred on by the conditions of colonial life. Isolation, the new environment, and economic growth all contributed to the inventiveness of European colonists in the New World. Moreover, the adventurous mindset that led people to try their chances in a new continent also led them to investigate their world and explore new ideas.

Innovation and Discovery

Isolated farming families had limited access to the latest tools and knowledge, but they encountered daily challenges in their new environment. By necessity they became inventors, fashioning tools for themselves out of the materials that were available to them. Necessity also required them to be their own physicians, trying whatever cures they could as disease or injury threatened their lives. City people, though less isolated, could specialize in a particular trade or craft, improving techniques as

they attempted to increase their productivity. Wealthy colonists, anxious to show that they were as educated as their European counterparts, kept in touch with the latest scientific theories emanating from European cities and joined the scientific debate.

The lives of colonial Americans were dominated by the hours of hard work it took to provide the necessities of life. During the eighteenth century, however, technological advances helped to make some of these tasks easier, such as lighting fires and candles, spinning wool into yarn, and hunting. Some of these advances originated in Europe but were eagerly adopted by Americans who recognized their importance. Other improvements were developed by the colonists themselves.

The Introduction of Matches

Candles and lamps were the only sources of artificial light in the eighteenth century. To light candles, people had to use tinder boxes—metal boxes filled with wood shavings and other flammable materials that were kept constantly smoldering. Tinder boxes, however, were troublesome and dangerous.

After the American Revolution Thomas Jefferson journeyed to France, where he saw matches for the first time. He realized immediately the usefulness of this new invention. Besides making it easier to light a candle, a match would also help melt the wax used to

Science, Technology, and Health **63**

The Beginnings of Mass Production

In the eighteenth century, factories that mass produced items had not yet been developed. Instead, goods were produced individually by artisans working alone or with a few assistants. Even small components like nuts and bolts were not interchangeable. They were crafted one at a time, and no two parts had identical dimensions. Instead of assembling a product from parts that had already been made, a gunsmith would make each gun individually. If the gun needed repairs, there were no available parts that would be certain to fit it.

Among the papers that date from the 1780s, when Thomas Jefferson was ambassador to France, is a description of the first steps toward mass production (quoted in Wendell D. Garrett's *The Worlds of Thomas Jefferson*). Jefferson immediately saw the advantages of this new way of manufacturing, and wanted his countrymen to be aware of the technique.

"An improvement is made here in the construction of the musket which it may be interesting to Congress to know. . . . It consists in the making every part of them so exactly alike that what belongs to any one, may be used for every other musket in the magazine. The government here has examined and approved the method, and is establishing a large manufactory for the purpose. As yet the inventor has only completed the lock of the musket on his plan. He will proceed immediately to have the barrel, stock, and their parts executed in the same way. Supposing it might be useful to the U.S., I went to the workman, he presented me the parts of 50 locks taken to pieces, and arranged in compartments. I put several together myself taking pieces at hazard as they came to hand, and they fitted in the most perfect manner. The advantages of this, when arms need repair, are evident."

seal a letter. In a letter to James Madison, Jefferson explained the expedience of matches:

> By having them at your bedside with a candle, the latter may be lighted at any moment of the night without getting out of bed. By keeping them on your writing table, you may seal three or four letters with one of them, or light a candle if you want to seal more which in the summer is convenient.[38]

Advances in Yarn Making

The time-consuming work of spinning sheep fleece into yarn so that it could be woven into cloth was reduced by the changes that occurred in producing a small but very important tool, the card. Obtaining cloth and clothing was always difficult for the colonists, as countless letters and diaries show. Technological progress even in a tool as small as the card contributed to the colonists' ability to produce yarn that could be woven into fabric.

After a sheep is shorn, the wool is in the form of fleece, a dense, tangled mat of hair. Someone holding a card in each hand would comb out the tangles of a small piece of the fleece, straightening the wool and forming it into a neat roll that could be spun. The card had a handle and a wooden back covered with a piece of leather that had many bent wires poking through it to comb the yarn. In the early days, to make a card the leather was pierced by hand with an awl. Then a length of wire was cut, slightly bent, set into the hole, and clinched in place. Each card had hundreds of wire "teeth." Later two machines were invented: One could cut and bend thirty-six thousand pieces of wire in an hour; the other pierced the leather backs.

The hand work involved in making a card was reduced again by a machine that performed all of the operations involved in cutting the wire and setting it into the leather. The time saved in making this essential tool allowed colonists to devote more time to the spinning itself, thus becoming more productive.

The Development of the Rifle

Colonists living in the countryside depended on hunting for a large portion of their meat. They needed rifles that were both accurate and light enough for them to carry through the backwoods. In the mid–eighteenth century, European rifles were still clumsy and heavy. They used heavy ammunition, were slow to fire, and produced a strong recoil. American colonists, however, had modified the rifle until it was lighter, longer, and more accurate. The ammunition it used was half the weight of European ammunition. Americans had also improved their loading technique

During the eighteenth century, women spent many hours spinning wool into yarn (left). The invention of the card helped speed this time-consuming process. Another technological advancement was an improved rifle, designed and manufactured in the American colonies (below).

through the use of the "patch." This small piece of greased cloth was wrapped around the lead ball, which could then be pushed smoothly down the barrel of the rifle. By making the ball fit tightly into the barrel, the patch improved the rifle's firepower. An Englishman traveling in Maryland in 1775 wrote that "rifles, infinitely better than those imported, are daily made in many places in Pennsylvania."[39] These improved firearms would play a pivotal role in the War of Independence.

Technology Connects to Science

American colonists also applied their practical knowledge to what is now called pure science. Americans took great interest in the astronomical and physical discoveries that were being made rapidly at this time by European scientists.

David Rittenhouse of Philadelphia built and improved on an intricate mechanism called an orrery, which was capable of displaying the positions of the heavenly bodies at any given time, five thousand years into the past or the future. Rittenhouse wrote about his plans for this device: "I would have my Orrery really useful, by making it capable of informing us, truly, of the astronomical phenomena for any particular point of time; which I do not find that any Orrery yet made, can do."[40] Americans were abandoning the superstitious fear of "portents" when they observed a comet or an eclipse and were moving instead toward a scientific ability to predict them. Rittenhouse's orrery provided a dynamic and flexible approach to understanding the orbits of the planets and other heavenly events.

Another Philadelphian, Benjamin Franklin, is famous for "discovering" electricity. In fact, he was fortunate to survive his experiment with the kite string and the metal key that he sent aloft to test his ideas about lightning. Others at the time were also interested in electricity, and some even speculated that it might have medicinal properties. What Franklin did achieve was proof of his brilliant theory: Electricity is a "single fluid," occurring in two forms, which he called "plus" and "minus."

With his kite, Franklin proved that lightning and electricity are identical and, as he wrote in his scientific journal, "the electrical fluid is attracted by points." From this realization, his creative but practical mind conceived the lightning rod:

> If these things are so, may not the knowledge of this power of points be of use to mankind, in preserving houses, churches, ships, &c. from the stroke of lightning, by directing us to fix on the highest part of these edifices, upright rods of iron made sharp as a needle, and gilt to prevent rusting, and from the foot of those rods a wire down the outside of the building into the ground, or down round one of the shrouds of a ship, and down her side till it reaches the water?[41]

Technological advances tended to have their detractors in the colonies, but gradually the changes won acceptance. Franklin's lightning rod found its way to roofs and steeples across the colonies, but naysayers argued that it was actually attracting lighting to the buildings, not channeling it safely to the ground. When a severe earthquake shook the city of Boston, the Reverend Thomas Prince gave an antitechnology interpretation of the event in a sermon:

> The more points of Iron are erected around the Earth, to draw the electrical substance out of the Air, the more the

Benjamin Franklin discovered electricity through an experiment involving lightning and a kite. The knowledge Franklin gained in this experiment led to the invention of the lightning rod that saved many homes and buildings from destruction by lightning.

Earth must needs be charged with it. . . . In Boston are more erected than anywhere else in New England; and Boston seems to be more dreadfully shaken. O! there is no getting out of the Mighty Hand of God! If we think to avoid it in the Air, we cannot on the Earth: Yes, it may grow more fatal.[42]

In spite of these dire predictions, it eventually became clear that Franklin's gilded rods were saving houses, barns, and churches from being struck and burned by lightning bolts.

Botany and Herbal Remedies

As colonial inventors harnessed the forces of nature to protect buildings from lightning, colonial scientists began exploring the natural world for cures to certain diseases. In the eighteenth century, the study of botany was closely allied with medicine since the most common medicines were derived from plants. Botanical treatises, known as "herbals," described plants, explained where and how they grew, and what medical applications they had. The New World provided opportunities for physicians trained in botany to catalogue a range of new flora.

In the early part of the eighteenth century, Mark Catesby published his *Natural History of Carolina, Florida, and the Bahama Islands*, which described a number of therapeutic plants that were new to European physicians, including mayapple, ginseng, witch hazel, and the "toothache tree." John Bartram founded the first American botanical garden near Philadelphia in 1725. He traveled widely in search of plants, adding specimens to his garden and sending specimens to English botanists with whom he corresponded.

Botanical Exploration of the Colonies

The Quaker naturalist John Bartram traveled extensively through the American wilderness with his son, William, who shared his father's appreciation for the natural world and for Native Americans. William became famous for his beautiful paintings of plants and animals. The Seminoles named him "Flower Hunter." Beginning in 1773 William made a four-year expedition, which he described in *Travels Through North and South Carolina, Georgia, East and West Florida,* excerpted from editor George McMichael's *Anthology of American Literature.* Though his travels in uncharted territory identifying and collecting botanical specimens were motivated by scientific inquiry, his reaction to the landscape around him was very emotional.

"Having completed my Hortus Siccus [collection of dried plant specimens], and made up my collections of seeds and growing roots, the fruits of my late western tour, and sent them to Charleston, to be forwarded to Europe, I spent the remaining part of this season in botanical excursions to the low countries, between Carolina and East Florida, and collected seeds, roots, and specimens, making drawings of such curious subjects as could not be preserved in their native state of excellence.

During this recess from the high road of my travels, having obtained the use of a neat light cypress canoe . . . I resolved upon a trip up the Alatamaha [river in Georgia].

I ascended this beautiful river on whose fruitful banks the generous and true sons of liberty securely dwell, fifty miles above the white settlements.

How gently flow thy peaceful floods, O Alatamaha! How sublimely rise to view, on thy elevated shores, yon Magnolian groves, from whose tops the surrounding expanse is perfumed, by clouds of incense, blended with the exhaling balm of the Liquidamber, and odours continually arising from circumambient [surrounding] groves of Illicium, Myrica, Laurus, and Bignonia."

Medical Advances: Inoculation Against Smallpox

The plants of the New World provided new types of medicines; nevertheless, in the eighteenth century colonial people began to suffer increasingly from epidemics of infectious diseases that no physician could cure. The spread of these epidemics was related to the differences between American and European cities. Even the largest American colonial cities were sparsely settled compared to the teeming cities of Europe, so diseases were less likely to spread from person to person. As the years passed, more and more Americans escaped infection, and the populace as a whole began to lose its immunity. The most deadly of these epidemic diseases was smallpox.

Historians believe that smallpox was endemic in England. In other words, almost everyone living there was exposed to it as a child. All adults were either immune or had acquired immunity by surviving a mild case of the disease in a process that was similar to modern Americans' experiences with measles or chicken pox. However, once Europeans settled in the New World, they were less likely to be exposed in this way to smallpox. As a result, when an infected person arrived in one of the colonies from Europe, the disease became an epidemic: Many people caught a severe form of the disease, and a high percentage of them died.

The Native Americans, who had no natural immunity, were devastated by smallpox, which sometimes killed half of a tribe in a few weeks. By the mid–eighteenth century, smallpox was sweeping through the white population as well, about once a generation or every twenty-five years. Boston, with its tightly packed houses, saw particularly severe outbreaks. Cotton Mather, the Puritan minister, read about inoculation as practiced in Turkey in the *Transactions of the Royal Society of London*, the leading scientific publication of the time, and wrote to a doctor there:

Puritan minister Cotton Mather made a huge medical contribution to the colonies by encouraging the people living in the city of Boston to be inoculated against smallpox.

How does it come to pass, that no more is done to bring this operation into experiment & into Fashion—in England? When there are so many Thousands of People, that would give many Thousands of Pounds, to have the Danger and Horror of this frightful Disease well over with them. I beseech you, syr, to move it [make it happen], and save more Lives. . . . For my own part, if I should live to see the Small-Pox again enter into our City, I would immediately procure a consult of our Physicians, to Introduce a Practice, which may be of so very happy a Tendency.[43]

When a West Indian ship brought some passengers with smallpox to the city soon thereafter, Mather tried to persuade Boston's physicians to try inoculation. The procedure was very dangerous, and conservatives made strong objections. But most of the arguments against the new idea were stated in theological or theoretical terms. The new approach was finally accepted and Dr. Zabdiel Boyleston (John Adams's great uncle) was able to inoculate three hundred people. Mather reported the results to the Royal Society: Only six of the inoculated patients had died. Five thousand other Bostonians caught smallpox, and of these, nine hundred died. This was the first instance in the European world of a disease being recognized and cured.

During the American Revolution, the movement of troops throughout the countryside brought smallpox infection to all of the colonies. On the advice of the chief physician of the army, George Washington had each soldier inoculated. Special hospitals were built for this purpose. Smallpox returned again to Boston in 1792, and twenty thousand people were inoculated. By the end of the century, the disease was no longer a major threat to the American people.

John Adams Is Inoculated

John Adams and Abigail Smith had set their wedding plans when, in 1764, a smallpox epidemic broke out in Boston. Abigail could keep relatively safe at her home in Weymouth, but John, as a lawyer, rode the circuit from courthouse to courthouse and was at high risk for infection. He did not want to take any chances of bringing the disease home to his fiancée, so he decided to be inoculated.

Unlike vaccination, inoculation involved actually infecting the patient with what was hoped to be a mild form of the dreaded disease. John obediently went through the prescribed regime, which involved ipecac to make him vomit, in preparation for the actual inoculation. In his letter to Abigail, whom he called by the pet name Diana, he took a light tone, probably to calm her fears as much as his own. This letter is excerpted from L. H. Butterfield's *The Book of Abigail and John.*

"My dear Diana

For many Years past, I have not felt more serenely than I do this Evening. My Head is clear, and my Heart is at ease. Business of every Kind, I have banished from my Thoughts. My Room is prepared for a Seven Days' Retirement, and my Plan is digested for 4 or 5 Weeks. My Brother retreats with me, to our preparatory Hospital, and is determined to keep me Company, through the Small Pox. . . . I have considered thoroughly the Diet and Medicine prescribed me, and any other fear from the small Pox or it's Appurtenances, in the modern way of inoculation I never had in my Life.

Sunday Morning—The People are all gone to Meeting, but my Self, and Companion, who are enjoying a Pipe in great Tranquillity, after the operation of our Ipechac. Did you ever see two Persons in one Room Iphicichuana'd together? (I hope I have not spelled that ineffable word amiss!) I assure you they would make merry diversion. We took turns to be sick and to laugh. When my Companion was sick I laughed at him, and when I was sick he laughed at me. Once however and only once we were both sick together, and then all Laughter and good Humor deserted the Room. Upon my word we both felt very sober. But all is now easy and agreeable."

The spirit of exploration that had brought Europeans to the New World did not die out as the newly discovered continent became colonized. Rather, the same spirit inspired new generations of immigrants to come to North America and to find ways of making a living in a strange environment. Once here, they encountered Native Americans whose culture had been shaped by the North American environment over countless generations.

CHAPTER 7

Encountering the Native Americans

When colonization began the eastern seaboard of North America was inhabited by many Native American peoples, but historians link them into four groups according to the type of language they spoke. In the northeast, the tribes spoke Algonquian languages. Siouan peoples inhabited the area that was to become the Carolinas. South of them were Muskogeans, and inland were Iroquoian peoples. Within each of these groups were numerous nations, each individually governed and varying widely in dialect and culture. Though they were sometimes joined in loose confederacies, these nations did not see themselves as a united group of "Indians," as the Europeans did. The Native American nations were often at war with one another, disputing the territory in which they hunted and fished.

Competing Civilizations

Perceiving their own way of life as superior, English colonists expected Native Americans to be impressed by their clothes, houses, and farm animals and to be curious about their religion. They were astonished that Native Americans did not choose to adopt the English way of life. As the Boston preacher Cotton Mather wrote,

> Tho' they saw a People Arrive among them, who were Clothed in *Habits* of much more Comfort and Splendour, than what there was to be seen in the *Rough Skins* with which they hardly covered themselves; and who had *Houses full of Good Things*, vastly out-shining their squalid and dark *Wigwams;* And they saw this People Replenishing their *Fields*, with *Trees* and with *Grains*, and useful *Animals*, which until now they had been wholly strangers to; yet they did not seem touch'd in the least, with any *Ambition* to come at such Desireable Circumstances, or with any *Curiosity* to enquire after the *Religion* that was attended with them.[44]

The native people of North America belonged to cultures that valued sharing more than personal possessions. They were not interested in the Europeans' display of wealth. Furthermore, the idea of "using" animals was alien to Indians. Respect for the natural world and the animals it contained formed part of most Native American belief systems. These and other values were taught by Indian families to their children, but most of the colonists, with their heritage of formal, organized religion, saw the native peoples as completely lacking in spiritual beliefs.

Whites in Indian Society

What was yet more astonishing to most colonists was the fact that large numbers of English people chose to live as Native Americans. Some of these people were captured

Some American colonists preferred the simpler life of the Native Americans and joined Indian tribes.

by Native Americans but did not attempt to escape their captivity, even refusing to return home when they were rescued. Other whites ran away from colonial society to join Indian society. Cadwallader Colden, a New York government official at the time, describes what happened when a peace treaty was made with the Indians and their captives were allowed to return home:

> No Arguments, no Intreaties, nor Tears of their Friends and Relations could persuade many of them to leave their new *Indian* Friends and Acquaintances; several of them that were by the Caressings

of their Relations persuaded to come Home, in a little Time grew tired of our Manner of living, and run away again to the *Indians*, and ended their Days with them.[45]

In addition, Colden said that Native Americans who had been raised in a colonial lifestyle never fully adopted it. Instead, they returned as soon as they could to their Indian way of life:

> *Indian* Children have been carefully educated among the *English*, cloathed and taught, yet, I think, there is not one

Instance, that any of these, after they had Liberty to go among their own People, and were come to Age, would remain with the *English*, but returned to their own Nations, and became as fond of the *Indian* Manner of Life as those that knew nothing of a civilized Manner of living.[46]

Benjamin Franklin was also puzzled that Indian life proved so attractive while "civilization" did not. In a letter to his friend Peter Collinson, he discussed the Indian attitude toward European society:

They visit us frequently, and see the advantages that Arts, Sciences, and compact Society procure us, they are not deficient in natural understanding and yet they have never shewn any Inclination to change their manner of life for ours, or to learn any of our Arts; When an Indian Child has been brought up among us,

Learning by Gaining an "Indian Ear"

When John Heckewelder traveled as a missionary among Native Americans, he tried to learn their languages. In his *Account of the History, Manners, and Customs of the Indian Nations, Who Once Inhabited Pennsylvania and the Neighbouring States,* Heckewelder described his difficulties. Heckewelder's account is reprinted in editor Newton D. Mereness's *Travels in the American Colonies.*

"When I first went to reside among the Indians, I took great care to learn by heart the words *Koecu k'delloundamen yun?* which mean *What do you call this?* Whenever I found the Indians disposed to attend to my enquiries, I would point to particular objects and repeat my formulary, and the answers that they gave I immediately wrote down in a book which I kept for the purpose."

However hard he tried, though, Heckewelder could not grasp the complex relationships between Native American words. "Those who are not acquainted with the copiousness of the Indian languages, can hardly form an idea of the various shades and combinations of ideas that they can express. For instance, the infinitive

Mitzin, signifies *to eat,* and so does *Mohoan.* Now although the first of these words is sufficiently expressive of the act of eating something . . . yet the Indians are very attentive to expressing in one word what and how they have eaten, that is to say whether they have been eating something which needed no chewing, as pottage, mush or the like, or something that required the use of teeth. In the latter case, the proper word is *mohoan,* and in the former *guntamen.* . . .

At last there came an Indian, who was conversant with the English and German, and was much my friend. I hastened to lay before him my learned collection of Indian words, and was very much astonished when he advised me immediately to burn the whole, and write no more. 'The first thing' said he, 'that you are to do to learn our language is to get an Indian *ear,* when that is obtained, no sound, no syllable will ever escape your hearing it, and . . . the rest will come of itself.' I found he was right. By listening to the natives, and repeating the words to myself as they spoke them, it was not many months before I ventured to converse with them and finally understood every word they said."

taught our language and habituated to our Customs, yet if he goes to see his relations and makes one Indian Ramble with them, there is no perswading him ever to return, and . . . when white persons of either sex have been taken prisoners young by the Indians, and lived a while among them, tho' ransomed by their Friends, and treated with all the imaginable tenderness to prevail with them to stay among the English, yet in a Short time they become disgusted with our manner of life, and the care and pains that are necessary to support it, and take the first good Opportunity of escaping again into the Woods, from whence there is no reclaiming them.[47]

Becoming a White Indian

A number of Europeans were taken captive by Native Americans who were following a cultural tradition of kidnapping an outsider to replace a tribe member who had died. Accounts of their experiences, written by several whites who were adopted, explain how the Native Americans welcomed their captives into their way of life and encouraged them to become "white Indians."

In many cases, one of the first things the Native Americans did for their European prisoners was to give them moccasins to wear on the journey into the wilderness. After enduring their pinching, hard-heeled shoes, the prisoners noted how much easier it was to travel through the woods in the soft, comfortable moccasins. If there was deep snow, the Native Americans would make snowshoes for their captives. These were unknown to the colonists, who were impressed by the Indians' ability to live in the wilderness. In addition, the Native Americans shared what little food they had equally with their prisoners. The colonists began to realize that they were not going to be treated

The Williams family follows their Indian captors into the wilderness. Although taken against their will, Indian captives were often treated well and encouraged to enjoy life as "white Indians."

harshly or as second-class citizens in Native American society.

Initiation Rites

Some Indians taught their captives songs as they led them along the trail to their village. The careful rehearsal of these songs was a preparation for a dance ceremony. One English woman, probably familiar only with restrained minuets, described the energetic dance she was taught by her captors:

> Little did we expect that the accomplishment of dancing would ever be taught us, by the savages. But the war dance must now be held; and every prisoner that could move must take its awkward steps. The figure consisted of a circular motion round the fire; each sang his own music, and the best dancer was the one most violent in motion.[48]

Once they reached the Native American village that was to be their new home, the European prisoners underwent three initiation rites. The first involved running a gauntlet of Indians who beat them with ax handles and tomahawks as they raced by. Some captives reported having been badly hurt in this ritual, but others said that they were not harmed. Barbara Leininger and Marie LeRoy, who were captured in Pennsylvania, wrote that the ritual beating was "administered with great mercy . . . merely in order to keep up an ancient usage, and not with the intention of injuring us."[49]

The next step in the captives' introduction to Native American life was a ritual washing. A prisoner named James Smith recalled that he was frightened when three Native American women led him into the water,

thinking they would drown him. However, one of the women spoke some English and told him he would not be hurt. "On this," Smith wrote, "I gave myself up to their ladyships, who were as good as their word; for though they plunged me under water and washed and rubbed me severely, yet I could not say they hurt me much."[50]

Finally the prisoners were dressed in Indian clothes and decorated with feathers, jewelry, and paint. With the whole village assembled around the council fire, the chief then welcomed the Europeans, announcing that they were now members of Indian society, equal with their captors. James Smith recorded the chief's words as they were translated for him by an interpreter:

> My son, you are now flesh of our flesh and bone of our bone. By the ceremony that was performed this day, every drop of white blood was washed out of your veins. You are taken into the Caughnewaga nation. . . . After what has passed this day you are now one of us by an old strong law and custom. My son, you have now nothing to fear. We are now under the same obligations to love, support and defend you that we are to love and defend one another. Therefore you are to consider yourself as one of our people.[51]

Native American Life

Once the initiation ceremonies were complete, captives were fully included in Native American life. They received gifts from their new families, and many were encouraged to marry. They were free to come and go as they wished, and they were taught Native American skills so that they could live and work as full members of Native American society.

Indian Ceremonies

General James Oglethorpe was commander in chief of the British forces in Georgia and South Carolina, where the colonists felt threatened by the Spanish in Florida. He found that the Spanish were trying to make the Indians of Georgia their allies in the struggle against the British colonists. Oglethorpe traveled among the Indian tribes, winning their trust and insuring their friendship. One of the Rangers in Oglethorpe's party wrote about their experiences in *A Ranger's Travels with General Oglethorpe, 1739–1742* (reprinted in Newton D. Mereness's *Travels in the American Colonies*). He described the elaborate welcoming ceremonies the British encountered in an Indian town.

"We Encamped about two miles from the Indian Town, The Indians sent Boys and Girls out of their Town with Fowls, Venison, Pompions [pumpkins], Potatoes, Water Melons, and Sundry other things. About ten of the Clock we set forward for the Indian Town and were met by the Indian King and some of their Chiefs, the King had English Colours [the English flag] in his hand. We Saluted them and they Returned our Salute, and then shaking Hands with the General and Company the King very gracefully taking him by the Arm led him towards the Town, and when we Came there they Brought us to Logs which they had placed for that purpose Covered with Bear Skins and desired us to sit down which when we had done The head Warriours of the Indians brought us black Drink in Conkshells which they presented to us and as we were drinking they kept Hooping and Hallowing as a Token of gladness in seeing us. . . . Afterwards we went to the Kings House or rather Hut where we Dined, at night we went to the Square to see the Indians dance, They dance round a large Fire by the beating of a Small Drum and Six Men singing; their Dress is very wild and frightfull their Faces painted with several sorts of Colours their Hair cut short (except three Locks one of which hangs over their Forehead like a horses for Top) they paint the Short Hair and stick it full of Feathers, they have Balls and rattles about their Waist and Several things in their Hands, Their Dancing is of divers Gestures and Turnings of their Bodies in a great many frightfull Postures."

As in white society, Native American men and women had distinct roles. The men spent most of their time fishing, hunting, or making war. They also made the tools and weapons. The women and children planted and harvested corn, pounded it, and made it into bread. They also made pots, baskets, and cooking tools. Women raised the children, who were, in the eyes of Europeans, undisciplined, disobedient, and disrespectful of their parents. The gentle, undemanding treatment of Native American children contrasted strongly with the practices the colonists had brought with them from Europe.

Giving and Sharing

Another cultural difference was that Native Americans had far fewer personal possessions than the colonists. Europeans established their status in society by what they owned—land, rich clothing, and fine horses and carriages. Native Americans, however, demonstrated their wealth and their position in society by what they could give to others. Consequently, the exchange of gifts was of great ceremonial and diplomatic importance among native peoples.

During the years he spent among Native Americans, missionary John Heckewelder came to understand better than most colonists the Indians' attitude toward land and their obligation to share:

> They think that [the Lord of all] made the earth and all that it contains for the common good of mankind; when he stocked the country that he gave them with plenty of game, it was not for the benefit of a few, but of all. Every thing was given in common to the sons of men. Whatever liveth on the land, whatsoever groweth out of the earth, and all that is in the rivers and waters flowing through the same, was given jointly to all, and every one is entitled to his share. From this principle, hospitality flows as from its source. With them it is not a virtue but a strict duty. Hence they are never in search of excuses to avoid giving, but freely supply their neighbour's wants

Squanto, a Wampanoag Indian, teaches the American colonists to grow corn. The Native Americans were able to teach colonists many tasks important to their survival.

from the stock prepared for their own use. They give and are hospitable to all, without exception, and will always share with each other and often with the stranger, even to their last morsel.[52]

The hospitality of Native Americans, even toward strangers, was what saved the Pilgrims during the harsh winter of 1620, when half of their number died. Samoset and Squanto, Wampanoag Indians, gave the survivors food and taught them to farm, fish, and hunt in the unfamiliar territory around Plymouth Plantation. The support of many Native American nations was also important later, during the wars fought in the New World until 1760. Indian warriors, guides, and scouts were active in both the British and French armies as well as the Spanish garrisons. The colonists relied on the help of some tribes, and feared the attacks of others, especially on the frontier farms.

Native American Government

The native peoples whom the colonists encountered lived in villages ranging from one hundred to perhaps a thousand people. Each village was led by a chief, who might receive a share of the game from a hunt, but was otherwise expected to fend for himself, even to the extent of making his own clothes. Although Algonquian villages remained largely independent, several chiefs would periodically hold a tribal council.

Some Native American leaders tried to establish centralized authority over a number of tribes. Powhatan had built up the Powhatan chiefdom in the Chesapeake region in the early 1600s. During the mid–eighteenth century, the Ottawa leader Pontiac brought together the Ottawa, the Pottawatomie, and the

Ojibwa in a loose confederation to resist British incursion into their lands. The Iroquois League was a closer union that united the Mohawk, Onondaga, Seneca, Oneida, and Cayuga nations. Charles Thomson, a colonial government official, studied the political organization of the Iroquois and described it for Thomas Jefferson. Thomson spent so much time among the Indians that the Delaware nation adopted him as a full member.

The great chief Powhatan established a coalition of several tribes in the Chesapeake region.

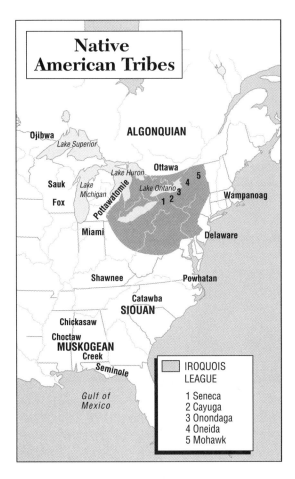

Native American Tribes

Ojibwa
Lake Superior
ALGONQUIAN

Sauk
Fox
Lake Michigan
Pottawatomie
Ottawa
Lake Huron
Lake Ontario
4 5
3
1 2
Wampanoag

Miami
Delaware

Shawnee
Powhatan

Catawba
SIOUAN

Chickasaw

Choctaw
MUSKOGEAN
Creek
Seminole

Gulf of Mexico

IROQUOIS LEAGUE

1 Seneca
2 Cayuga
3 Onondaga
4 Oneida
5 Mohawk

According to Thomson's description, each Iroquois village built a council house where local decisions were made and where delegates to the tribal council were elected. The tribal council in turn elected delegates to the national council. Thomson explained that the leaders—or sachems—were elected to, rather than inherited, their positions. He pointed out that outsiders adopted into the nation could even be elected to office.

Learning from Native American Culture

As they began to see themselves as a nation rather than a series of dependent colonies,

the Europeans of North America drew on the example of the Iroquois. The idea of a confederation of colonies did not come from Europe, where nations guarded their borders closely. It may have been the Iroquois chief Canassatego who first suggested that the colonies unite into a federation. He pointed to the league of the Iroquois as an example of how the colonies could form one nation without having to give up their own sovereignty. Benjamin Franklin urged his fellow colonists to adopt the Iroquoian system of government, and the U.S. Constitution includes many elements drawn from the Indian confederation.

The founders of the United States also drew on Native American tradition when they envisioned a democracy based on equality among all men. The democracies that had developed in Europe still extended voting rights only to a small class of privileged landowners. Native American society showed the colonists a way of life where power was not restricted to a small ruling class. The concept of impeachment also came from Indian culture. In Europe a monarch ruled until death, but a Native American sachem who lost the confidence of his tribe could be voted out of office by tribe members.

The Clash of Cultures

In spite of the importance of this heritage, the story of the encounter between European and Native American cultures is, overall, a tale of loss and sorrow. The powerful, technologically advanced immigrants soon found their way through the wilderness that had so frightened the Pilgrims when they landed on Cape Cod. As the whites built their cities, towns, and farms, they created a society that welcomed hundreds of thousands of other Europeans to follow in their footsteps. With guns, military power, the practice of owning and fencing land, and the custom of working together to build united governments, whites simply overpowered the native peoples of North America.

Native American life was transformed, and not entirely for the better, as traditional crafts—and the roles of the Native craftsmen—disappeared due to preference for the products of European technology. Tribes over-hunted deer and other animals to obtain deerskin and furs to trade with the colonists for the objects they wanted. This process disrupted traditional patterns of life and increased the Indians' dependence on white settlers. In addition, relationships with neighboring nations were damaged, sometimes leading to crippling wars. Yet it is easy to understand why someone would prefer an iron pot to a container made of birch bark or a glass bottle to a drinking gourd. Iron-edged tools soon took the place of the axes, spears, and arrowheads that had been laboriously chipped from flint.

Some of the harm to native peoples resulted from chance events, and some from

Indians established a fur trade with colonists in order to trade for manufactured items that saved them time and effort.

Native Americans generally valued European clothing and adopted pieces of it when they could. Captain John Smith, in *The Generall Historie of Virginia, New England, and the Summer Isles*, recorded what the Indians in Virginia had worn before they obtained garments made of woven cloth. This excerpt is taken from Diana de Marly's *Dress in North America*.

"For their apparell they are sometimes covered with the skinnes of wild beasts, which in Winter are dressed with the hayre [hair], but in Summer without. The better sort weare large mantels of Deereskins, not much differing in fashion from the Irish mantels. Some imbroidered with white beads, some with Copper, others painted after their manner. But the common sort have scarce to cover their nakedness but with grasse, the leaves of trees or such like. We have seen some use mantels of turkey feathers, so prettily wrought and woven with threads that nothing could be discerned but the feathers. That was exceedingly warm and handsome.

But the women were always covered about their middles with a skin and are very shame faced to be seene bare. They adorn themselves most with copper beads and painting. The women, some have their legs, hands, breasts and face cunningly imbroidered with divers workes, as beasts, serpents, artificially wrought into their flesh with black spots.

In ech eare commonly they have three great holes whereat they hang their chains, bracelets or copper. Some of the men weare in these holes a small greene and yellow coloured snake, neare a half a yard in length, which crawling and lapping herself about his necke oftentimes familiarly would kiss his lips."

choices made by individuals or groups. Tribes were decimated both by European diseases, to which they had no resistance, and by the loss of their traditional hunting grounds. Settlers were pressing farther and farther into what they saw as wilderness, populated only by small bands of nomadic people who could, in the eyes of the whites, simply move farther west. With their traditions of land ownership and the establishment of permanent farms, European settlers had no appreciation for the size of the territories needed by each Indian nation for hunting and raising crops in the different seasons of the year.

As they moved away from being "subjects of His Majesty" the king of England and strove to become independent citizens of a new nation, white settlers gradually shed some of the European ways they had inherited from their forebears and took on important elements of Native American culture. The peoples who lived along the east coast of the United States prior to the Europeans' arrival have since vanished, but their values and attitudes played a significant role in the development of the American nation.

Life in the New World

The Englishmen who originally settled the American colonies were confident in their possession of traditional rights—the "liberties, franchises and immunities" guaranteed in their charters. Their goal in governing their new communities was to retain the laws and customs by which their families had lived for generations. Yet their experiences in the colonies made fundamental changes in their lifestyle, in their relationship to the English crown, and in the way they saw their world.

The first need was for survival, and the second need was for adjustment to the constant changes brought by successive waves of immigrants and by the rapid growth of the colonial economy. By the mid–eighteenth century the colonists had met and sur-

mounted these imperatives and, in the process, developed a distinct national character. Independent and self-reliant, some colonists foresaw a change in their relationship to Great Britain. Political thinkers like Benjamin Franklin speculated that the balance of power would change. Possibly King George would move to the New World and center his kingdom there!

The wars that had raged in so many parts of the colonies were now concluded, but peace had several unexpected consequences. Many colonists had traveled widely as they participated in the English armies. These experiences gave them a wider perspective and helped them gain a sense of identity with people from other colonies. The English, however, had a different reaction to their ex-

General Braddock leads his soldiers to battle during the French and Indian War. Colonial soldiers gained a broader perspective and sense of unity from their experiences.

As an expression of their desire for freedom, American colonists pull down a statue of King George. Colonists' desire for independence led them to loosen their ties with England.

periences during the wars in the New World. They saw the general prosperity of the colonies and observed how different this was from the poverty that was all too common at home. In addition, England now had enormous American territories to govern. It needed tax money to pay for maintaining the English empire along the greatly expanded American frontier.

The Advantages of the Situation

The colonists, on the other hand, saw the frontier as an opportunity. They felt that they had made a significant contribution to winning the conflicts with the French and the Spanish, and they saw no further responsibility for support-

ing the British government. It was in this atmosphere that Parliament, with no colonial members, began imposing a series of taxes that had harsh consequences for both the colonial economy and ordinary people.

These unwelcome evidences of imperial power stood in sharp contrast to the colonists' growing sense of self-reliance and ability to take independent action when a challenge arose. The New Englanders' experience in running town affairs, the planters' ability to create self-sufficient farming communities, and the wealthy merchants' ability to buy and sell with many nations prepared the colonists to loosen their ties to Europe. As George Washington argued,

> If we remain one people, under an efficient government, the period is not far

off when we may defy material injury from external annoyance; when we may take such an attitude as will cause the neutrality we may at any time resolve upon to be scrupulously respected; when belligerent nations, under the impossibility of making acquisitions upon us, will not lightly hazard the giving us provocation; when we may choose peace or war, as our interest, guided by justice, shall counsel.

Why forego the advantages of so peculiar a situation? Why quit our own to stand upon foreign ground? Why, by interweaving our destiny with that of any part of Europe, entangle our peace and prosperity in the toils of European ambition, rivalship, interest, humor, or caprice?[53]

People living in the new culture of the colonies did not feel part of the old rivalries between European nations. The independent inhabitants of the colonies were losing their sense of being "subject" to the English king.

In the New World, perceptive European Americans had also gained a different perspective on the design of government as they observed Native American styles of leadership. Here they found a model for interdependence in which separate nations could build associations that preserved the rights of each member. Here was a possibility for government built on mutual interest rather than dominance. The colonists were beginning to see that their interests lay with each other, not with fealty to a foreign crown. Their challenge would be to create a new world order in which they could work with and support each other.

Notes

Introduction: Becoming Americans

1. Quoted in Daniel J. Boorstin, *The Americans: The Colonial Experience*. New York: Random House, 1958.
2. Quoted in Stephanie Grauman Wolf, *As Various as Their Land: The Everyday Lives of Eighteenth-Century Americans*. New York: HarperCollins, 1993.
3. Quoted in Boorstin, *The Americans*.
4. Quoted in Richard Middleton, *Colonial America: A History, 1585–1776*. 2nd ed. Oxford: Blackwell, 1996.
5. Quoted in Middleton, *Colonial America*.
6. Quoted in Middleton, *Colonial America*.

Chapter 1: Immigrant Societies and Communities

7. Quoted in Boorstin, *The Americans*.
8. Quoted in George McMichael, ed., *Anthology of American Literature*. Vol. 1. New York: Macmillan, 1974.
9. Quoted in Richard Hofstadter, *America at 1750: A Social Portrait*. New York: Knopf, 1971.
10. Quoted in Hofstadter, *America at 1750*.

Chapter 2: Living in a Colonial City

11. Quoted in Wilson Smith, ed., *Cities of Our Past and Present: A Descriptive Reader*. New York: Wiley, 1964.
12. Quoted in McMichael, *Anthology of American Literature*, vol. 1.
13. Quoted in Thomas J. Wertenbaker, *The Golden Age of Colonial Culture*. New York: Great Seal Books, 1959.
14. Quoted in William L. Andrews, ed., *Journeys in New Worlds: Early American Women's Narratives*. Madison: University of Wisconsin Press, 1990.

15. Quoted in Wertenbaker, *The Golden Age of Colonial Culture*.
16. Quoted in Wertenbaker, *The Golden Age of Colonial Culture*.
17. Quoted in Wertenbaker, *The Golden Age of Colonial Culture*.
18. Quoted in Wertenbaker, *The Golden Age of Colonial Culture*.
19. Quoted in Middleton, *Colonial America*.

Chapter 3: Life in the Countryside

20. Quoted in McMichael, *Anthology of American Literature*, vol. 1.
21. Quoted in Wolf, *As Various as Their Land*.
22. Quoted in Wolf, *As Various as Their Land*.
23. Quoted in Wolf, *As Various as Their Land*.
24. Quoted in Wolf, *As Various as Their Land*.

Chapter 4: Home and Hearth

25. Quoted in Wolf, *As Various as Their Land*.
26. Quoted in Wolf, *As Various as Their Land*.
27. Quoted in McMichael, *Anthology of American Literature*, vol. 1.
28. Herbert Applebaum, *Colonial Americans at Work*. Lanham, MD: University Press of America, 1996.
29. Quoted in Wolf, *As Various as Their Land*.
30. Anna Green Winslow, *Diary of Anna Green Winslow*. Ed. Alice Morse Earle. Boston: Houghton, Mifflin & Co., 1895.
31. Quoted in Shirley Glubok, ed., *Home and Child Life in Colonial Days*. London: Macmillan, 1969.
32. Quoted in Andrews, *Journeys in New Worlds*.
33. Quoted in Diana de Marly, *Dress in North America, Volume 1: The New World, 1492–1800*. New York: Holmes & Meier, 1990.

Chapter 5: Crafts, Skills, and Professions

34. Quoted in Boorstin, *The Americans.*
35. Quoted in Boorstin, *The Americans.*
36. Quoted in Boorstin, *The Americans.*
37. Quoted in Boorstin, *The Americans.*

Chapter 6: Science, Technology, and Health

38. Wendell D. Garrett, *The Worlds of Thomas Jefferson.* New York: Weathervane Books, 1971.
39. Quoted in Boorstin, *The Americans.*
40. Quoted in Boorstin, *The Americans.*
41. Quoted in Boorstin, *The Americans.*
42. Quoted in Boorstin, *The Americans.*
43. Quoted in Boorstin, *The Americans.*

Chapter 7: Encountering the Native Americans

44. Quoted in James Axtell, "The White Indians of Colonial America," *William and Mary Quarterly*, vol. 23, 1975.
45. Quoted in Axtell, "The White Indians of Colonial America."
46. Quoted in Axtell, "The White Indians of Colonial America."
47. Quoted in Wilcomb E. Washburn, ed., *The Indian and the White Man.* New York: New York University Press, 1964.
48. Quoted in Axtell, "The White Indians of Colonial America."
49. Quoted in Axtell, "The White Indians of Colonial America."
50. Quoted in Axtell, "The White Indians of Colonial America."
51. Quoted in Axtell, "The White Indians of Colonial America."
52. Quoted in Washburn, *The Indian and the White Man.*

Epilogue: Life in the New World

53. Quoted in Boorstin, *The Americans.*

For Further Reading

L. H. Butterfield, *The Book of Abigail and John: Selected Letters of the Adams Family, 1762–1784.* Cambridge, MA: Harvard University Press, 1975. The letters written by Abigail and John Adams provide a window into the world of the mid–eighteenth century. They are full of stories, ideas, news, and insight into the minds of our country's founders.

Shirley Glubok, ed., *Home and Child Life in Colonial Days.* London: Macmillan, 1969. Combines two works written in the late nineteenth century by Alice Morse Earle and adds new illustrations of family life, children's pastimes and education, and many crafts and farming practices.

Cheryl G. Hoople, *The Heritage Sampler: A Book of Colonial Arts and Crafts.* New York: Dial Press, 1975. Each chapter of this book focuses on a craft, giving a short introduction followed by recipes or instructions for a project. Quilting, candle making, weaving, and butter making are among the topics it covers.

George McMichael, ed., *Anthology of American Literature.* Vol. 1. New York: Macmillan, 1974. In this book, McMichael excerpts Benjamin Franklin's *Autobiography*, Thomas Jefferson's *Notes on the State of Virginia*, and a variety of other colonial sources.

Richard Middleton, *Colonial America: A History, 1585–1776.* 2nd ed. Oxford: Blackwell, 1996. A clear, interesting history of colonial times written for adults. However, it has good maps, timelines, and illustrations to help make the events easier to understand.

Lila Perl, *Slumps, Grunts, and Snickerdoodles: What Colonial America Ate and Why.* New York: Seabury Press, 1975. Describes the dishes (such as succotash, snickerdoodles, and hush puppies) that evolved when the colonists encountered the foods of the New World and tried to adapt them to their tastes. Each chapter describes the origins of a specific dish and ends with a recipe.

Bernardine S. Stevens, *Colonial American Craftspeople.* New York: Franklin Watts, 1993. This book describes the skills of woodworkers, builders, metal workers, leather workers and other colonial craftspeople and the processes they used.

John F. Warner, *Colonial American Home Life.* New York: Franklin Watts, 1993. Describes the home life of colonists of all classes and origins as well as slaves and Native Americans. Chapters include: Colonies and Colonists, Homes, Clothing, Food, Work, School, Getting the News, Amusements, and Visiting Yesterday. Many of the illustrations appear to be later impressions of what colonial life was like rather than contemporary drawings or engravings.

Anna Green Winslow, *Diary of Anna Green Winslow.* Boston: Houghton, Mifflin, & Co., 1895. This book contains all of the diary pages that still existed when Alice Morse Earle borrowed them from a Winslow descendant to publish. Anna wrote about her friends, her church, her lessons, the housework that she did, her feelings, and her clothes.

Works Consulted

William L. Andrews, ed., *Journeys in New Worlds: Early American Women's Narratives.* Madison: University of Wisconsin Press, 1990. This book reprints four narratives written by colonial women in the eighteenth century, including Sarah Kemble Knight's *The Journal of Madam Knight.* It has helpful introductory essays explaining what is known about the authors and their lives.

Herbert Applebaum, *Colonial Americans at Work.* Lanham, MD: University Press of America, 1996. Many details on the world of work in the different regions and in the different industries and crafts.

James Axtell, "The White Indians of Colonial America," *William and Mary Quarterly,* vol. 23, 1975. This article explains a little-known fact of American colonial history: the Native American practice of kidnapping and adopting whites into their own cultures.

Daniel J. Boorstin, *The Americans: The Colonial Experience.* New York: Random House, 1958. This book illuminates the ideas and values of the people whose lives formed American culture.

Edward C. Boykin, ed., *The Autobiography of George Washington.* New York: Reynal and Hitchcock, 1935. This "autobiography" has been assembled by the editor out of excerpts from Washington's writings over his long and distinguished life.

Bill Bryson, *Made in America; An Informal History of the English Language in the United States.* New York: Morrow, 1996. Bryson's book is a light-hearted history of the English language in America from the colonial period to the present day.

Howard W. French, "The Atlantic Slave Trade: On Both Sides, Reason for Remorse," *New York Times,* April 5, 1998. New and valuable perspectives on the background of the slave trade and its effects on today's Africa.

Wendell D. Garrett, *The Worlds of Thomas Jefferson.* New York: Weathervane Books, 1971. This book presents excerpts from Jefferson's letters, journals, and government documents, along with photographs of the places and portraits of the people involved.

Richard Hofstadter, *America at 1750: A Social Portrait.* New York: Knopf, 1971. Detailed discussions of population, servitude, the slave trade, and life as a middle-class person in the American colonies. This book focuses on the colonists' thoughts and attitudes.

Diana de Marly, *Dress in North America, Volume 1: The New World, 1492–1800.* New York: Holmes & Meier, 1990. A very detailed description of the shoes, stockings, hats, wigs, and underwear, as well as dresses and suits, worn by American settlers and native peoples. Includes illustrations from contemporary art.

Newton D. Mereness, ed., *Travels in the American Colonies.* New York: Antiquarian Press, 1961. A collection of eighteen travel narratives written by a range of people, from colonels to missionaries, and covering many parts of the eastern seaboard and inland.

Vincent Scully, *American Architecture and Urbanism.* New York: Praeger, 1969. Scully discusses buildings in their urban contexts, as they exist together in a city, in a culture, and within a historical time period.

Amelia Simmons, *American Cookery*. Bedford, MA: Applewood Books, 1996. Reprint of the first cookbook in America.

Wilson Smith, ed., *Cities of Our Past and Present: A Descriptive Reader.* New York: Wiley, 1964. This book presents quotations from many different writers that give descriptions of American cities throughout history.

Robert Blair St. George, ed., *Material Life in America, 1600–1860.* Boston: Northeastern University Press, 1988. This book contains many articles on the way that colonial Americans lived and worked.

Wilcomb E. Washburn, ed., *The Indian and the White Man.* New York: New York University Press, 1964. A collection of documents designed to tell the story of the relationship between Native Americans and white settlers.

Jack Weatherford, *Indian Givers: How the Indians of the Americas Transformed the World.* New York: Crown, 1988. Includes the contributions to world cultures of Central and South American peoples as well as those of North American Indian nations.

Thomas J. Wertenbaker, *The Golden Age of Colonial Culture.* New York: Great Seal Books, 1959. A survey of housing, furniture, literature, music, plays, schools, and other aspects of life in colonial cities.

Stephanie Grauman Wolf, *As Various as Their Land: The Everyday Lives of Eighteenth-Century Americans.* New York: HarperCollins, 1993. Outlines many important issues in colonial life, with abundant quotations from a wide range of different people of the time.

Lewis B. Wright, *The Atlantic Frontier: Colonial American Civilization 1607–1763.* Ithaca, NY: Cornell University Press, 1947. A careful, detailed discussion of the nature and government of the early colonies.

Index

Account of the History, Manners, and Customs of the Indian Nations, Who Once Inhabited Pennsylvania and the Neighbouring States, 42, 73
accounting, 31
Adams, Abigail, 39, 43–44, 70
Adams, John, 38–39, 44, 49, 60, 69–70
Africa, 10, 20, 23
Africans, 11, 22, 24, 25, 50
Albany, New York, 17
Albemarle (province), 21
alchemy, 63
alcohol, 22
Algonquians, 71, 78
Allegheny Mountains, 8
ambergris, 31
American Revolution, 23, 39, 54, 59, 63, 69
ammunition, 65
Anabaptists, 28
Andrews, William L., 21, 28
Anglican Church, 15, 28, 59
Annapolis, Maryland, 21
Anthology of American Literature, 13, 18, 24, 33, 58, 68
Appalachian Mountains, 12, 45
apples, 40, 55
apprentices, 56–59
architecture of colonial cities, 31
Arctic, 10
artisans, 26, 56
arts in colonial cities, 36–37
Asia, 10
assault and battery, 60
astronomy, 35–36, 66
Atlantic Ocean, 11–13, 15
attacks by wild animals, 46
Autobiography (Franklin), 18,

29, 49
Aztecs, 12

banks, 31
Baptists, 59
Barbados, 21–22, 32
barns, 41, 67
barrels, 42, 45
barter system, 39
Bartlett, Josiah, 38
Bartram, John, 67–68
Bartram, William, 68
bears, 46
Bennett, Joseph, 28
Bethlehem, Pennsylvania, 46
blacksmiths, 59
bleeding, 61
Book of Abigail and John, The, (Butterfield), 39, 44, 70
bookstores, 36
Boston
　architectural style of churches in, 31
　Benjamin Franklin runs away from, 49
　bookstores in, 36
　as center of colonial thought, 37
　earthquake in, 66
　establishment of, 15
　fires in, 33
　Hancock Mansion in, 34
　improvement of streets in, 28
　John Franklin starts printing shop in, 58
　layout of, 27
　population of, 16–17, 26
　public schools in, 35
　slaves in, 23
　smallpox epidemic in, 69
botany, 60, 67–68

boundary disputes, 13
Bowery, 28
Boyleston, Zabdiel, 69
Braddock, General, 82
Bradford, William, 8
bread, 18, 76
Brewton, Miles, 34
bridges, 42, 46
British Empire, 26
Broadway, 37
Brown (college), 59
Burnaby, Andrew, 21
Burroughs, Mr., 28
butchering, 40
Butterfield, L.H., 39, 44, 70
Byrd, William, II, 48

Canada, 8
canals, 42
Canassatego (Iriquois chief), 79
candles, 31, 37, 40, 58, 63
Cape Cod, 79
cards (yarn-making tool), 64–65
Caribbean islands, 30
Carolinas, 11, 21, 68, 71
　see also North Carolina; South Carolina
carpenters, 45, 59
Catesby, Mark, 67
Catholics, 20–21, 30
cattle, 41
Cayuga Indians, 78
Central America, 12, 22
Chandler, Edward, 50
chandlery, 58
charcoal, 59
Charles II (King of England), 18
Charleston, South Carolina, 22, 24, 26, 32, 34–35, 37, 68
charters, 13

Chesapeake Bay, 20
Chesapeake region, 78
chickens, 34, 43
children in the colonies, 50–52, 76
China, 10
Christianity, 10, 22
Church of England, 28
churches, 15–16, 19, 21, 28, 31, 59, 60, 67
cities, life in, 26–37
    design of, 27
Clarendon (province), 21
clothing, 30, 39, 52–53, 64
coffee, 19, 55
Colden, Cadwallader, 72
College of Pennsylvania (University of Pennsylvania), 60
colleges, 59–60
Collinson, Peter, 73
Colonial America (Middleton), 14
Colony House, 29
Columbia (King's College), 60
commerce, 16, 29, 31, 57
concerts, 30
Congregationalists, 59
Connecticut, 10, 15–16, 21, 47, 59
Constitution, U.S., 79
construction, 57, 59
Continental Congress, 38, 43–44
cooking, 40, 42–43, 45, 54–55
Copley, John Singleton, 34
corn, 18, 21, 29, 40, 54–55, 77
corsets, 31, 52
cottage industries, 16
cotton, 23
countryside, life in, 38–47
cows, 34, 43
crafts, 16, 26, 34, 56–62
Crèvecoeur, Michel-Guillaume-Jean de, 13, 24
crops, 18, 19, 29–30, 38–41, 43, 60

Currency Act, 37

dancing, 35
Dartmouth (college), 59
Declaration of Independence, 44
Delaware (state), 17
Delaware Indians, 78
Delaware River, 18
"Descriptions of Charleston; Thoughts on Slavery; on Physical Evil; a Melancholy Scene" (Crèvecoeur), 24
Diary of Anna Green Winslow, 35, 52
diseases, 23, 63, 68
doctors, 56
domestic servants, 25
Dowes, Madame, 28
Dress in North America (de Marly), 81
Dutch Reformed Church, 59
Dutch settlements, 17

earl of Orrery, 48
earthquakes, 66
education, 34–36
eggs, 34, 43
electricity, 66
Elizabeth, New Jersey, 18
embroidery, 35
England, 13–15, 17, 30, 38, 58, 61, 68–69
English language, 35
Episcopal churches, 28
estates, 60
Europe, 10, 30, 37
explorers, 10
exports, 30, 40

factories, 63
family life, 48–55
Faneuil, Peter, 28
Faneuil Hall, 28–29
farmhands, 48
farming, 12, 16, 18–19, 21–22,

25, 38–47, 63
fashion, 52–53
fencing, 41, 45
firefighting in colonial cities, 33
fish, 31, 54–55
fishing, 12, 17, 30, 54, 71, 76
fleece, 64
Florida, 8, 68, 76
flour, 18, 29
food, 54–55
forests, 38, 41, 46, 59
fortifications, 47
Fox, George, 10–11
France, 13, 24, 37, 63
Franklin, Benjamin
    becomes apprentice in brother's print shop, 58
    comments about Indian attitudes, 73
    concerns of, about risk of fires in Philadelphia, 33
    describes interests of early colonies, 13
    describes workers in printing shop, 18
    discovers electricity, 66–67
    expresses prejudice against German colonists, 19
    as Indian Commissioner, 10
    marriage of, 49
    meets governor of Pennsylvania, 29
    opens first public libraries, 36
    views of, about Iroquoian government, 79
Franklin, John, 58
French and Indian War, 37, 82
French Church, 28
French language, 35
French settlements, 8
fur trade, 21, 80
furnaces, 59
furniture, 30, 39

gardening, 43, 45
Garrett, Wendell D., 61, 64
Generall Historie of Virginia, New England, and the Summer Isles, The (Smith), 81
George, King, 13, 82–83
Georgia, 21–23, 45, 53
Germantown, Pennsylvania, 19
Germany, 14
ginseng, 67
girdling, 41
Gnadenhutten, 42
Godfrey, Mrs., 49
gold, 10, 63
Governor's Palace, 29
Great Spirit, 42
Greek literature, 35–36
Green, the (central square), 27
Gridley, Mr., 60

Hancock Mansion, 34
handwriting, 35
Harris, Thomas, 46
Hartford, Connecticut, 16
Harvard, 59–60
harvesting, 43
heating, 42
Heckewelder, John, 42, 73, 77
herbal remedies, 67–68
herbs, 55
Higginson, Francis, 15
hogs, 34, 40–41
Holland, 31
"holy experiment," 18
hominy, 54–55
hopping John, 54
horses, 40, 42, 46
House of Burgesses, 21
houses, 41, 59, 67
Hudson River, 18
"humors," 61
hunting, 12, 38, 45, 54, 63, 71, 76, 80

immigrants
    communities of, 15–25

German-speaking, 18–19
    reasons for coming to New World, 9–10
Incas, 12
indentured servants, 11, 18, 20, 39–40
Independence Hall (State Hall), 28
India, 10
Indian corn, 18, 54
Indians. *See* Native Americans
indigo, 22, 40
initiation rites, 75
inoculations, 68–70
insurance, 31
ipecac, 70
Ireland, 30, 47
iron, 42
ironworks, 57, 59
Iroquois, 71, 78–79
Iroquois League, 78
itinerants, 38

Jamaica, 32
James River, 20
Jamestown, Virginia, 19, 57
Jefferson, Thomas, 38, 43, 45, 50, 60, 62–64
Journey to Pennsylvania (Mittelberger), 14
journeymen, 57
Journeys in New Worlds: Early American Women's Narratives, (Andrews, ed.) 21, 28

King's Chapel, 28
King's College (Columbia), 60
kites, 66
Knight, Sarah Kemble, 21, 28, 31, 52
knitting, 40, 43

laborers, 26, 34, 43, 59
lamps, 31, 63
Latin literature, 35–36
law, 36

lawyers, 53, 56, 59, 60–61
layout of colonial cities, 26–27
lead, 61
leather, 40
Leininger, Barbara, 75
LeRoy, Marie, 75
Letters from an American Farmer (Crèvecoeur), 13, 24
Lewis, John, 35
libraries, 36
lifestyles
    in cities, 26–37
    in the countryside, 38–47
    of families, 48–55
    of Native Americans, 75–76
lightning rods, 66
literature, 35
Livermore, Judge, 61
livestock, 39–41
London, 13, 18, 22, 31–32, 69
Long Island, 31
Louisiana territory, 8

Maine, 15, 30, 45
Manhattan, 17
Mannitto, 42
mansions, 31, 34, 55
maps, 46
Marblehead, Massachusetts, 16
maritime commerce, 57
Marly, Diana de, 81
marriage, 48–50
Maryland, 20–21, 23, 57, 66
masons, 45, 59
Massachusetts (state), 8, 10, 15–16, 21–22, 29, 59
Massachusetts Bay, 47, 54
Massachusetts Bay Company, 26
mass production, 64
masters of colonial workshops, 56–57
Mather, Cotton, 69, 71
Mayflower, 8
McMichael, George, 13, 18, 24, 33, 58, 68

meat, 29, 31, 34, 40, 43, 54–55
medicine, 30, 36, 60–62
Mein, John, 36
merchants, 26
Mereness, Newton D., 46, 73, 76
Middleton, Richard, 14
militias, 47
milk, 34, 40, 43
mills, 41–42
mining, 57
ministers, 56, 59–60, 62
missions, 59
Mississippi River, 8
Mittelberger, Gottlieb, 14
moccasins, 74
Mohawk Indians, 78
molasses, 29
Monticello, 43, 45
Montreal, 37
Moravians, 46
music, 35
Muskingum (river), 42
Muskogeans (Indians), 71

Native Americans
    beliefs of, 42
    colonists' encounters with, 71–81
    giving among, 76–78
    hostility of, toward colonists, 45
    John Bartram's appreciation of, 68
    population of, 12
    reject conversion to Christianity, 10
    sharing among, 76, 78
    smallpox epidemics and, 62, 69
    teach colonists to make native foods, 55
    teach girdling to colonists, 41
Natural History of Carolina, Florida, and the Bahama Is-
lands (Catesby), 67
navigation, 35–36
needlework, 35
Netherlands, 31
New Amsterdam, 17, 26, 30–31.
    see also New York (city)
Newark, New Jersey, 18
Newburyport, Massachusetts, 16
New Canaan, 26
New-Englands Plantation (Higginson), 15
Newfoundland, 30
New Hampshire, 10, 15–16, 38, 61
New Haven, Connecticut, 16, 21, 26–27
New Jersey, 17–18, 57
New Orleans, 8
Newport, Rhode Island, 29
New York (city)
    architecture in, 31–32
    layout of, 27
    naming of, 26
    plays in, 37
    population of, 17
    slaves in, 23
    see also New Amsterdam
New York (state)
    colleges in, 60
    farms in, 18
    fashion in, 52
    ironworks in, 57
    population of, 35
    as shipping center, 30
New York Mercury, 32
North Carolina, 21, 23, 46
northwest passage, 10
Nova Scotia, 35, 51–52

Oglethorpe, James, 76
Ojibwa Indians, 78
Old Amsterdam, 32
Old South Church, 62
Old World, 48, 60
Oneida Indians, 78
Onondaga Indians, 78
orchards, 40
orrery, 66
Orrery, earl of, 48
Otis, James, 37
Ottawa Indians, 78
Oxford, 18

Pacific Ocean, 10
panthers, 46
Parliament, 37, 61, 83
patroonships, 17
Penn, William, 18, 27, 29
Pennsylvania
    completion of Independence Hall in, 28
    founding of, 18
    governor of, meets Benjamin Franklin, 29
    as haven for religious sects, 10
    ironworks in, 57
    militias in, 47
    population of slaves in, 23
    requirements for holding government positions in, 19
    rifles made in, 66
perfume, 31
Philadelphia
    Benjamin Franklin and concerns about fire in, 33
    describes co-workers in, 18
    opens first public libraries in, 36
    as center of colonial thought, 37
    completion of Independence Hall in, 28
    creation of first botanical garden in, 67
    fires in, 33
    inventions by residents of, 66
    layout of, 27

naming of, 26
taverns in, 29
physicians, 43, 59, 61–63
pickled meat, 29
pigs. *See* hogs
Pilgrims, 8, 12, 15, 54, 78–79
planes, 59
plantations, 19–23, 25, 38, 40, 43, 45–46, 62
plays, 30
playwrights, 37
plowing, 40
plumbing, 28
Plymouth (town), 47
Plymouth Company, 8
Plymouth Plantation, 15, 78
Plymouth Rock, 8
Pontiac Indians, 78
ponytails, 54
popcorn, 55
population
  of Boston, 26
  of Charleston (South Carolina), 26
  of New York City, 26
  of slaves, 23–25
portraits, 34
Portsmouth, New Hampshire, 16
Pottawatomie Indians, 78
Powhatan (Indian chief), 78
Presbyterians, 59
prescriptions, 61
Prince, Thomas, 66
Princeton, 59
printing shops, 58
professions in colonies, 56–62
Providence, Rhode Island, 16, 23, 26
public libraries, 36
pumpkin, 55
Puritans, 15–16, 18, 36, 48, 59, 69

Quakers, 11, 18, 28, 47, 68

Ranger's Travels with General Oglethorpe, A, 76
religious persecution, 10–11, 18
Revere, Paul, 34
Revivalist Baptists, 59
Reynolds, John, 46–47
Rhode Island, 15–16, 29–30, 58
rice, 22, 25, 30, 40
rifles, 65–66
Rittenhouse, David, 66
rituals of Indians, 75
roads, 46
Rogers, Mr., 21
Rolfe, John, 19
Royal Society of London, 69
rum, 29
rye, 29, 40

Salem (Massachusetts), 16, 26
Samoset (Wampanoag Indian), 77
sawmills, 59
schools, 34–36
science, 63–70
seafood, 54
seaports, 30–31, 37
Seminole Indians, 68
Seneca Indians, 78
servants, 11, 18, 20, 24, 34, 39–40, 48–49
sewers, 28
sewing, 43
Shakespeare, 37
sheep, 40, 64
shipping, 20
shoes, 30, 45, 74
silversmiths, 34
Sioux Indians, 71
skilled craftsmen, 25
slaughtering, 42
slaves
  capture of, in Africa, 11
  clothing of, 53

food of, 31
inoculation of, against smallpox, 62
marriage and, 50
meals of, 54
population of, 12, 23–25
punishment of, 45
tasks of, 39
as workers on plantations, 20, 22–23, 43, 45
smallpox, 62, 68–70
Smith, Abigail. *See* Adams, Abigail
Smith, James, 75
Smith, John, 81
smokehouses, 55
snowshoes, 74
societies of immigrants, 15–25
South America, 10, 12, 22
South Carolina, 21–23, 32, 46
Spain, 30
Spanish settlers, 8, 76
spices, 55
spinning, 40, 45, 63–65
Squanto (Wampanoag Indian), 77–78
squash, 55
Stamp Act, 37
State House (Independence Hall), 28
state houses (stadt-houses), 21
steeples, 31, 66
stores, 59
streets of cities, 27–28
succotash, 55
Sudbury Street, 52
sugar, 21–22, 29, 40, 55
Sugar Act, 37
surveying, 36

tariffs, 13
taverns, 19, 29
taxes, 37
tea, 19, 55
teachers, 43
technology, 63–70

tenants, 38
Thacher, Thomas, 62
Thanksgiving, 51
theaters, 36–37
Thomson, Charles, 78–79
timber, 17
tinder boxes, 63
tobacco, 19–20, 22–23, 25, 43
tools, 59
toothache tree, 67
Transactions of the Royal Society of London, 69
traveling between colonies, 21, 46
Travels in the American Colonies, 42, 46, 73, 76
Travels Through North and South Carolina, Georgia, East and West Florida (Bartram), 68
Turkey, 69

University of Pennsylvania (College of Pennsylvania), 60

unskilled laborers, 26
vaccination, 70
venison, 54
Vermont, 15
Virginia, 19–23, 29, 43, 45–47, 48, 57, 59–60
Virginia Company, 8, 19

Wachovia, North Carolina, 46
wagons, 40
Walton, William, 36
Wampanoag Indians, 54, 77–78
War of Independence, 66
Washington, George, 62, 69, 83
waterwheels, 41
wealthy colonists, 34, 51, 63
weaving, 40, 45
West Africa, 22
West Indies, 11, 17, 29, 31–32
whaling, 17, 31
wheat, 18, 29, 54
white Indians, 74
wigs, 53–54
William and Mary (college), 59, 61

Williamsburg, 21, 26, 28, 37, 46
Williams family, 74
Winslow, Anna Green, 35, 51–52
witch hazel, 67
wolves, 41, 46
women
    fashion of, 52–53
    population of, in colonies, 50
    roles of, on farms, 42–43
    roles of Native American, 76
wood, 41–42, 59
wool, 45, 63
workshops, 56–57
Worlds of Thomas Jefferson, The (Garrett), 61, 64
writing, 35
Wythe, George, 61

Yale (college), 59
yarn, 63–65

Picture Credits

Cover photo: Scala/Art Resource, NY

Archive Photos, 23, 40, 49, 57, 60, 80

John Grafton, *The American Revolution*, Dover Publications, Inc., 1975, 27, 29, 45, 65 (right)

Historical Pictures Stock Montage, 20

Laura Greer Illustration & Design, 79

Library of Congress, 12, 36, 58, 67, 69, 72, 78, 83

North Wind Picture Archives, 11, 16, 17, 30, 32, 34, 43, 50, 51, 53, 54, 59, 62, 74, 82

Prints Old and Rare, 44

Stock Montage, Inc., 19, 33, 41, 65 (left), 77

About the Authors

Ruth Dean is the president of the Writing Toolbox in Akron, Ohio. She writes books and articles and does research projects for health care organizations. She has taught English composition and research writing at the University of Akron and worked as a tutor in its Writing Center.

Melissa Thomson has a doctorate from Trinity College, Dublin, and taught seventh grade before moving to the United States. She writes articles and reports for the Writing Toolbox and sings in Apollo's Fire, a music group in Cleveland, Ohio.